THE HOUND, THE HANGMAN AND OTHER HAUNTINGS:
a gazetteer of Welsh ghosts

The Hound,
the Hangman and other
Hauntings:

a gazetteer of Welsh ghosts

Thomas Corum Caldas

First published in 2010

© Thomas Corum Caldas

ISBN: 978-1-84524-170-4

Cover design: Eirian Evans

Published by Llygad Gwalch,
12 Iard yr Orsaf, Llanrwst, Wales LL26 0EH
tel: 01492 642031
fax: 01492 641502
email: books@carreg-gwalch.com
internet: www.carreg-gwalch.com

Contents

Note: the names of all living persons mentioned in this book have been changed.

Introduction

I was about three years old when I saw my first ghost, a beautiful lady dressed in white. She stood in the corner behind the wood-burner in my parent's bedroom. My brother, who was in the same room, was completely unaware of her presence. Was the incident just a figment of my imagination? Was it a trick of the light that the vivid mind of a young child quickly transformed into a person that seemed to be made of flesh and blood? This is at least what many critics have given me as an explanation. Even as an adult I still maintain that the lady in white really appeared in my parent's bedroom, and that I had the privilege of seeing her, whereas my brother was insensitive to her presence. This observation is in keeping with paranormal science. Research work has revealed that somebody can live in a haunted place without being aware of the haunting whereas another person can come along and feel the presence of the ghost all at once.

Since my childhood I have had various encounters with ghosts. Generally speaking the ability to sense the presence of the supernatural seems to run through my family. My paternal grandmother saw several ghosts during her lifetime.

I spent many years in Ireland where I became a member of an ancient druidic order. I was trained in the craft of the druids, which also included teachings on the nature of ghosts. The scientific approach of the order clashed somewhat with the romantic ghost tales and personal experiences of my childhood. I learned that the nature of a ghost cannot be defined so easily. A ghost is commonly described in English dictionaries as a disembodied spirit of a dead person that appears to a living person or persons. In reality the subject is far more complicated because a large number of apparitions are of living people, or rather, of people who are alive when they appear to the general public although they are on the verge of dying. The appearance of a dying person to the living is known as crisis manifestation in paranormal research.

It has been argued that ghosts are nothing but recordings in some kind of a magnetic field in the building substance of a building similar to a recording on a video tape. If given only superficial consideration this explanation sounds plausible enough. Upon closer inspection there must be much more to this theory. There are cases in which the original building substance has completely disappeared and yet the haunting continues in the successor building! Spectres also show themselves frequently in the countryside where there has never been a building to begin with.

When we see a deceased relative or friend in a dream it is still a haunting, according to the definition found in English dictionaries. It is still a dead person that appears to the living. That the experience happens in a dream is inconsequential. What matters is why the dead relative or friend appears in the dream. Does the spirit insert itself in the dream or does the dreamer subconsciously draw on his memories of the departed relative? If indeed a ghost is the disembodied spirit of a deceased person that appears to the living, as suggested in English dictionaries and encyclopedias, what then are we to make of the appearance of a phantom coach? A vehicle made of wood and metal is hardly likely to have a spirit that appears to the living and yet there are innumerable ghostly coaches that show themselves to the living.

I have chosen not to include true poltergeist phenomena in this book because many of these incidents seem to be centered around the living rather than the dead as, for instance, in the famous case of a poltergeist haunting at a lawyer's office in Rosenheim in Germany where the supernatural occurrences appeared to be linked to one of the employees. Going into the nature of poltergeist phenomena would far exceed the scope of this book.

The book was written to acquaint the reader with haunted places in Wales which still exist and can be visited. While the book was never meant to be a heavy work of science that slays the reader with theories it still conveys a basic scientific understanding of the nature of a haunting. For this reason the book is both informative and readable. While the book gives an abundance of facts and details it can still be read for pleasure.

Ghosts are variously also called apparitions, spirits, spectres, shades and phantoms. These expressions are freely used in the book to avoid repetition. Some of these synonyms go back to older languages. Thus the modern English word 'phantom' has its roots in 'phantasma', which is a Greek word for 'ghost'.

The book is also a tribute to the unfortunate victims of cruelty mentioned in the text – like poor Lady de Clare, who was buried up to the neck in a field – or victims of immuration and so forth. The pages of this book point an accusing finger at their torturers and murderers.

Dear reader, enjoy reading the book, but just to be on the safe side have a rosary ready and some holy water, as well as several pointed stakes and the phone number of a good exorcist. Well, to be sure, a Bible sometimes works wonders, and not to mention the rites of the druids. Maybe you are not even aware of the seven foot tall skeleton that stands in the corner near your fireplace or looms over you when you lie in your bed taking your pleasant sleep ...

Thomas Corum Caldas
Swansea, 2010

1

Pubs, inns and hotels

Old inns and pubs often have a fascinating history. In bygone centuries, for example, smugglers, pirates and robbers frequently used inns as safe meeting places and store houses. This tradition is especially remembered in literature such as *Treasure Island* where the Admiral Benbow becomes the haunt of a fearsome pirate. His presence attracts a number of even more terrifying characters. In Falkner's *Moonfleet* the Why Not Inn is the hideout of a gang of smugglers. In order to keep prying eyes away from the loot, their leader deliberately spreads rumours about a ghost that haunts the area where the gang hides their contraband.

In periods that were rife with superstition such rumours would probably have worked efficiently. There is reason to suppose that a number of accounts of supernatural phenomena in pubs or inns can be traced to a similar wish to fend off unwelcome attention.

Nonetheless, the history of many pubs and inns deviates from that pattern, and they can therefore be regarded as truly haunted. Places where droves of people have met over the years provide an ideal background for tragic events, which in turn may lead to a haunting. Anybody who has a love for the supernatural or likes a bit of a thrill may feel tempted to investigate a particular haunting. After all it is not every day that one can have a drink in such interesting company.

Most of the spectral lodgers in the pubs and inns of Wales

are quite harmless, but there are also a few mischievous or even harmful phantoms around, such as, for instance, at the Llindir Inn in Henllan, where a spectral sea captain sometimes assaults the visitors, or the phantom of the Rummer in Cardiff, which causes a feeling of great dread.

Aberdare *(Aberdâr)*, Rhondda Cynon Taf
The mischievous ghost of the Conway Inn
The ghost of the Conway Inn in Aberdare is not harmful, but is of a mischievous and playful nature. One could almost be led to believe that the ghost suffers from ennui and attempts to find relief from this boredom by plaguing the occupants of the inn with its pranks.

The spectre has never shown itself to anybody, but the impish creature always finds a way to let the residents know that it is definitely there. Sarah, the niece of the owner, has had a few encounters with it. While away for a month her uncle left Sarah in charge of the inn. One night a loud bang that came from the taproom awakened her. Sarah was not frightened. As the burglar alarm had not gone off she knew there was no intruder in the house. But when she checked out the taproom in the morning she discovered that a chair near the main door had been knocked over. A more detailed search revealed that a number of bottles had been thrown about during the night.

If Sarah had been the only one to experience an inexplicable occurrence at the inn one would be inclined to believe that the disturbance was due to a natural cause. However, even clients feel uncomfortable in certain parts of the building. The top of the stairs and the women's toilet are especially affected by the haunting. Numerous patrons have felt a presence in these parts of the inn.

Abergavenny *(Y Fenni)*, Monmouthshire
The haunted stairwell of the King's Arms
The ghost of the Kings Arms in Abergavenny differs greatly from the noisy and invisible spirit in the previous story. The phantom loves to be clearly visible. Over the years a good number of clients have noticed a ghostly woman dressed in black clothes.

She was first seen in 1970, which does not necessarily mean that the spectre was not present before that date. Sometimes the presence of a ghost is kept secret for fear of negative publicity. The age of the lady in black is roughly known. She has been described as elderly. The woman in black usually appears on the staircase of the pub. Quite like an ordinary person she simply walks down the stairs and traverses the lounge of the Kings Arms. If she did not vanish all of a sudden she could easily pass for a person of flesh and blood.

Abergele, Conwy
From the graveyard to the Bull Hotel
Inns and hotels often provide homes for more than one ghost. The Bull Hotel in Abergele has three resident ghosts.

Sometimes the ghost of a young monk manifests itself in the building. Little is known about the fate of the monk. Some source material gives the monk's death as accidental. It is said that the monk slipped on a wet surface and fell, injuring himself seriously. He died as a result of his injuries. The premature death of the monk may be the cause of this particular haunting.

A former resident of the hotel, a young man who died in a motor bike accident, frequently appears to the visitors. His remains rest in a graveyard nearby. The sad ghost is always dressed in a black motor bike suit.

From time to time the shade of a young unidentified

woman wanders around in the building. The cause of her death is unknown.

The hotel is also haunted by spooky noises, ghostly cold spots, phantom smells and eerie shadows.

Aberystwyth, Ceredigion
The hovering ghosts of the Clarendon Hotel

The ghosts in the previous two accounts range from boisterous to sad. One can only guess at the pain the motorcyclist whose ghost frequents the Bull Hotel must have felt at the moment of his death. It is therefore not surprising that his mournful shade keeps returning to his former home. Yet, a haunting does not always have to be either tragic or boisterous. As the following story will show it can be of a rather romantic nature.

A married couple from Shropshire, John Abbot and his wife, stayed at the Clarendon Hotel in Aberystwyth on 23 July 1971, and experienced a haunting.

Sleep did not come easily to Mrs Abbot that night. She thought that some fresh air might do her good. Mrs Abbot opened a window and watched the promenade in front of the hotel. For a while she observed a young lady who was leaning against the railing of the promenade, apparently watching the sea. After some time another stranger appeared on the promenade, a young man who came running down the road. This was, so it seemed, an everyday occurrence. Suddenly Mrs Abbot realised that the two young people were not actually walking or standing but floating in the air at the height of about a foot from the ground.

Profoundly shocked, Mrs Abbot awakened her husband and hastily informed him about what had occurred. Mr Abbot rushed to the window and was as shocked as his wife when he saw the two young strangers hovering in the air. By then the ghostly girl had become aware of the approaching young man and turned to greet him. Then they lovingly embraced one another. The couple seemed happy enough. After a while the two ghosts turned on the spot and ran up the promenade. They walked down a set of steps and crossed the beach only to walk right into the returning tide.

Since then a number of local people have confirmed that the promenade in front of the Clarendon Hotel is haunted.

Afonwen, Flintshire
The spectral monk of the Pwllgwyn Hotel

The Pwllgwyn Hotel, like the Bull Hotel, is the last home of a spectral monk.

The hotel is steeped in history. Long ago pilgrims used to stay at the hotel on their way to St. Winifred's Well. Monks and nuns would have constantly been around the place. It is therefore not unusual that the ghost of a monk should haunt the building. Dressed in a habit, he can frequently be seen in the dining room of the hotel, sitting at a table just like an ordinary client, lost in thought. The monk is so real and substantial that he is often taken for a customer of flesh and blood.

The ghost of an unknown man sometimes appears in the taproom. The landlord of the cosy hotel in Afonwen first noticed the spectral tenant early one morning when he entered the taproom. At that time of the day the taproom was still closed to the public. The landlord had no explanation as to how the stranger had accessed the taproom. He was even more amazed when the stranger vanished before his eyes. The landlord searched every inch of the area but found no trace of the stranger. Later in the day the landlord had another encounter with the ghost. He was reading at a table in the taproom when he suddenly noticed the ghost standing at the bar. Once again the ghost vanished before the landlord's eyes.

A phantom woman sometimes shows herself in one of the upstairs rooms. She is linked with some mischievous occurrences that trouble this particular room. The landlord once stood at a table in that room when he felt a hand slipping into his pocket. He instantly turned round and was surprised to find that he was the only person in the room.

Babell, Flintshire
The loutish ghost of the Black Lion
While the haunting the Conway Inn in Aberdare is boisterous and merry, one of the ghosts at the Black Lion in Babell must be classified as harmful. A number of witnesses reported being attacked by the spirit. The attacks usually take the form of a slap on the backside. Both barstaff and customers have experienced the ghost's rough treatment. The spectre especially likes assaulting the users of the lady's toilet. The identity of the ghost has so far remained unknown.

The pub also has a mischievous ghost that makes its presence felt in numerous unpleasant ways. One of the ghost's preferred pranks is to knock over bottles. Despite its loutish behaviour the ghost seems to have a considerate nature, as it takes care not to break any of the bottles it knocks over.

On another occasion the ghost showed itself to a patron. Above the bar in the taproom of the pub there is an impressive ornament, an iron mask. Lost in thought, the patron was looking at the mask when all of a sudden a face appeared in it. As the man cried out in shock the glass in front of him inexplicably shattered.

A few days after the incident in the taproom the witness returned with his wife for a good night out. The night passed uneventfully, but when the couple was about to leave the haunting struck again. While the man was saying his goodbyes his wife sat on her own near the side door. The door handle began to move and rattle and the door was pushed open but nobody entered. The wife checked the area and found out that nobody had been there.

All this pales compared to what the daughter of a former owner of the Black Lion experienced while she lived there. She frequently saw an unknown woman sitting on her bed. It soon dawned on her that the visitor was a ghost.

Even the cellar of the Black Lion is said to be haunted. The saying is that the spirits of Roman legionaries wander around in the cellar rooms. Investigators should listen carefully: they may be able to hear the clinking of armour and the footfall of sandal-wearing feet. While it cannot be promised that a visitor will hear the blaring sound of ancient Roman horns, catching a few words spoken in harsh and husky Latin is always possible. What is more, the blood-curdling groaning of the legionaries when they received their fatal wounds may still linger around in the cellar. Enjoy your visit.

Bargoed, Caerffili
The Hallowe'en ghost of the Emporium Snooker Club
The ghost of the Emporium in Bargoed is neither mischievous nor harmful, nor is it awe-inspiring like the spectres of the legionaries in the previous story. Its character is completely different. One could go as far as to say that the ghost has a certain sense of humour.

One night two friends, Jason and Richard, spent a few hours at the Emporium playing snooker. Jason will probably never forget that evening. He witnessed a haunting.

Jason and Richard entered the Emporium through a little door near the car park. They walked down a narrow staircase which led to the reception area where they used another set of stairs to access the main snooker hall. Once there Jason immediately prepared the snooker table while Richard rushed back up to the car park to fetch his 'lucky chalk' from his car. After he had retrieved his chalk he remained in the car park and phoned his mother. He was in a hurry to get back and thus did not speak with his mother for much longer than five minutes.

In the meantime Jason was busy setting up the snooker balls, which took him only a few moments. When he had completed his task he lit up a cigarette and began to wonder what was keeping Richard so long. Smoking relaxedly, he looked around the snooker hall and noticed a woman in black near the toilets. In a strange and inexplicable way Jason felt attracted to the woman in black and began to study her closely. After a little while he concluded that there was something strange about her. He found that the woman looked more like a witch out of a fairytale than a customer of a snooker hall. As the light was quite dim Jason could not make out whether she wore a black dress or a top with a skirt. Anyway, the front of her skin-tight clothes was adorned with many buttons. The lady in black, quite like a traditional witch, also wore pointed ankle boots. She was rather tall and slim and her hair was caught up in a bun on top of her head.

The Black Lady walked from the toilets to the very flight of stairs Jason and Richard had used only moments ago. Jason watched her attentively as she climbed the stairs. Just as she disappeared behind a corner on the stairs Richard emerged from there. The lady in black must have inevitably passed him on her way up. However, to Jason's great amazement Richard did not respond to the jokes he made about the woman with the spooky appearance. It was only when Richard told his friend that he did not know what he was talking about that Jason realised that something was horribly wrong. Richard finally explained that he had never seen the lady in black. At this point it dawned on the two men that Jason had seen a ghost, and what a ghost! The lady in black apparently loves to don her Hallowe'en finery when she shows herself to a witness. This betrays a certain class and style and a good sense of humour!

Barry (Y Barri), Vale of Glamorgan
The phantom lady of the Royal public house
The female ghost that haunts the Royal pub in Barry certainly lacks the sense of humour of the lady in black at the Emporium. The most that can be said of her is that her behaviour may be slightly indecent at times as she tends to manifest herself in the gents' toilet. Other than that she appears to haunt all parts of the building and shows herself to both staff and patrons alike.

The phantom woman seems to be quite harmless. She never threatens or attacks anybody. It is rather her unexpected appearances in the most unlikely locations of the building that frighten those who meet her. Once a patron, John, had a close encounter with the ghost in the male toilet. He was surprised to see a woman standing in the gents' toilet, near the sink. Upon closer inspection the woman seemed unearthly and spooky. Quite disconcerted, John rushed back into the taproom and informed the landlady of his brush with the ghost. The landlady was not at all surprised and as if it were the most common occurrence in the world she pointed out that John had only seen the ghost of the pub.

John is not the only one to whom the ghost appeared. A former member of staff, Kelly, who used to work and live at the pub, witnessed the woman on numerous occasions.

Unfortunately, so far it has not been possible to establish the identity of the ghost, nor is it known why the woman haunts the pub.

Beddgelert, Gwynedd
Royal Goat Hotel
There are various reasons that can cause a haunting. They range from hidden treasure to a violent death. The death of the monk and that of the motorcyclist at the Bull Hotel serve as illustrating examples. The trade of the ghostly Roman

legionaries at the Black Lion was of a violent nature and accordingly they also died a violent death. As strange as it may sound, happiness can sometimes be the cause of spectral activity. Even stranger than that is that the fabrication of a story may be the reason that keeps the ghost of David Pritchard on earth.

Mr Pritchard, the former landlord of the Royal Goat Hotel in Beddgelert and spinner of tales, haunts the hotel he once owned. There his ghost still walks through the hallways and can often be seen. As to why he has remained earth-bound we can only guess. Was it his love for wealth and money that now compels him to haunt the Royal Goat Hotel? Or was it, as some researchers suggest, the tale of Gelert, the faithful hound, which may be a fabrication that made him so restless?

All its life Gelert served his master prince Llywelyn faithfully. One day Llywelyn went on a hunting trip. He was away from home for a number of hours. On his return he found his faithful dog covered in blood. He also noticed that the cradle that contained his young son had been knocked over. This left only one conclusion open: Gelert had killed Llywelyn's infant son. In a fit of anger the prince drew his sword and slew the hound. When he turned over the cradle to retrieve the dead body of his son he discovered that the child was actually alive and well. The blood on Gelert had come from quite a different source. Next to the child the prince found the carcass of a wolf. It then dawned on prince Llywelyn that his faithful dog had been wounded and bloodied defending the infant.

Critics have pointed out that the folktale of Gelert may be of recent origin, a tale invented by Pritchard to attract more trade to his establishment. Pritchard would have had access to foreign source material, as 'faithful hound' stories can be found all over the world.

It has therefore been suggested that lies and greed keep the ghost of Mr Pritchard in his former home.

Bodfari, Denbighshire
The elegant lady ghost of the Dinorben Arms

Ghostly ladies dressed in black are a frequent occurrence, but one should not leap to the conclusion that they have stereotype personalities. The witchy lady in black at the Emporium has an impish and comical touch to her personality, whereas the woman in black that haunts the Dinorben Arms in Bodfari is of a rather different nature: she is majestic, as shall be seen.

The pub stands on a site that was formerly occupied by a Roman villa. Most historical sites have almost inevitably been the scene of tragic events, incidents that have left the spirits of the departed restless. Accordingly several spirits have remained behind at the Dinorben Arms. The haunting was particularly noticed in the late twentieth century.

A spectral woman in black often shows herself in the building. Both clients and staff have seen her on numerous occasions. We therefore have a relatively detailed description of her physical characteristics. Her hair is long and dark and she invariably wears a sweeping black dress which gives her a regal and elegant appearance. She prefers to haunt the upper floors of the pub. A former employee, Owen, had an encounter with her at the end of his shift. One Friday evening he was last to leave the upstairs restaurant. On his way out he suddenly noticed the ghostly lady. She came out of the kitchen and walked to the restaurant, where Owen lost sight of her.

The ghosts of a man and a child have also been seen. Is there a link between these two ghosts and the lady in black? Did they know one another when they were alive? Were they maybe in a family relationship? If so, does the cause of the haunting originate in a family tragedy? Be it as it may, the three ghosts are benevolent. Nobody has ever felt uncomfortable in their presence. This cannot be said of the fourth spectral being that haunts the Dinorben Arms, the Uncanny Watcher.

Several witnesses have complained about an invisible presence that followed them around the building. The ghostly entity never seemed to leave them. They felt constantly spied upon by invisible eyes. The Uncanny Watcher strikes mostly in the upstairs rooms of the pub.

Disembodied voices and strange noises are part of the haunting. So far it has not been possible to establish whether these noises are caused by any of the known ghosts of the Dinorben Arms.

Caernarfon
The haunted taproom of the Anglesey Arms
The area around the Anglesey Arms has a sinister history. Right next to the building executions were once carried out in the Hanging Tower. The tower still exists. The inn itself began its life as a customs house and is reputed to be haunted in all parts. Although there is no concrete evidence, it is tempting to connect the haunting with the presence of the neighbouring Hanging Tower. It is quite conceivable that the atmosphere of despair and gloom left behind by those who suffered and died in the tower has spread to the inn.

The haunting is most noticeable in Room 3, where visitors have complained about an entity that sat on the bed. Because of the visible presence of a ghost, the spectral occurrences in Room 3 appear to be somewhat outstanding. Yet this does not mean that the rest of the inn is free of uncanny phenomena.

In the taproom, glasses are often moved about by some invisible force. Sometimes they even hang in mid-air as if suspended from invisible strings. A barman once had first-hand experience with the ghost and gave a detailed description. He saw a glass on a six-foot-high shelf moving around on its own accord. It eventually fell from the shelf, but miraculously survived the fall unharmed. Here again it can be argued that the ghost is playful rather than malicious. The spectre shows respect for private property by not breaking it.

The local darts teams has also felt the power of the haunting. Quite often it is impossible to finish a game of darts in peace. The mischievous ghost interferes. In a leisurely way the ghost makes the darts drop from the board. The players have our sympathy. It must be somewhat annoying when one has just hit the bull's-eye but the hit does not count. But then again, nobody has ever said that it is easy to live with a ghost.

Caernarfon
The strangler of the Black Boy Inn
The haunting of the Black Boy Inn may very well be similar in nature to the spook of the Anglesey Arms, where the adjacent area appears to play an important role. The assumption that the Hanging Tower exerts a certain influence on the neighbouring inn cannot be rejected out of hand. Similarly, it must be taken into consideration that the Black Boy once formed part of Caernarfon's red-light district. It is therefore logical to assume that the prostitutes of the area frequented the inn. The haunting of the Black Boy may consequently be connected with the unhappy lives of many of the prostitutes. The area around the inn was probably rife with theft and violence.

Quite in keeping with the above mentioned theory a female ghost has been seen in the taproom. Sally Thomas, who works for the Black Boy, explained in a video interview conducted by the *Caernarfon Herald* that a manager had an encounter with a ghostly woman late one night when he was on his own in the inn. Sally explained that the manager was still visibly shocked in the morning. The witness statement of a single individual could be doubted, but fortunately, the manager has some support, as another member of staff has also seen the ghost. This female witness must have somehow found out the identity of the ghostly woman, as she sometimes refers to the ghost by name: Martha. Martha seems placid and benevolent enough, something which cannot be said of the other ghosts that haunt the inn. The nickname of one of them reflects the violent nature of the spook. This particular ghost is known as 'the strangler'.

The strangler attacks both visitors and staff. It never shows itself. This ghostly entity acts as an invisible presence that causes a strangling feeling just as if a pair of hands closed around a person's neck. Given the history of the area it does not come as a surprise that a phantom strangler should be active in it. After all, Whitechapel suffered from the Ripper, so maybe there was once a strangler in the red-light district of Caernarfon.

Yet another ghost seems to be drawn to a particular bedroom in the building. The spectre is not necessarily of a violent disposition. Nonetheless the ghost is best to be avoided unless one is very brave: without fail, everyone that has come across it has described it as quite scary.

Cardiff *(Caerdydd)*
The phantom of the Rummer Tavern
The haunting of the Rummer in Cardiff follows the pattern explored in the article on the Dinorben Arms. An invisible and uncanny watcher spreads a feeling of discomfort at the Dinorben Arms. The Rummer is also troubled by an uncanny watcher. The difference here is that this particular haunting appears to be far more forceful.

The Rummer Tavern looks back on a long history. It is known that the pub was granted its first licence as early as 1713. With its old oak beams and much wood panelling the pub has preserved the atmosphere of bygone centuries and not only that: it is haunted.

On a Friday in October 2000 Jack and a friend paid a visit to the Rummer Tavern to enjoy an evening out. After a while

Jack went to the toilet. When he entered the toilet he could clearly see that he was alone in the room. Yet when he stood in front of the urinal he had the distinct feeling that somebody was standing behind him. Several times he looked over his shoulder but failed to see anybody. The feeling of being watched by an invisible entity sent waves of fear through Jack. He began to believe that he was in grave danger. When he washed his hands he noticed a reflection in the mirror above the basin. When he turned around he caught sight of something that was of human size. Before Jack could clearly identify who or what it was, it disappeared.

Visibly shaken, he related the event to his friend. The friend readily believed Jack and went to see for himself. Although he did not have an encounter with the mysterious ghost he still felt the feeling of fear and oppression.

Gareth Rogers, who works for the *South Wales Echo*, investigated the haunting of the Rummer Tavern, and his report was printed on 29 August 2007. According to the article the manager of the Rummer, Mr Melbourne, and his staff are well aware of the haunting, which is largely centred around the ladies' toilet and the cellar. Mr Melbourne also explained that he once had a brief encounter with a phantom man who wore a white shirt.

A possible explanation for the origin of the haunting maybe found in a legend connected with the pub. Long ago a seaman caught his wife in bed with her lover. Some time after the incident he died, consumed with jealousy and anger. The shade of the angry sailor is said to haunt the pub. It would make sense to link the sailor with the uncanny watcher in the toilets. The husband of an unfaithful wife would have a good reason to be watchful.

The manager believes that contrary to what has been said and written, their ghost is friendly because it has never harmed anyone.

Chepstow *(Cas-gwent)*, Monmouthshire
A lady in grey at the St. Pierre Golf and Country Club
St. Pierre is another building with a lady haunting. The phantom lady of St. Pierre differs from previous accounts in that she prefers to dress all in grey instead of black. The lady in grey is thought to be a deceased family member.

St. Pierre once belonged to Sir David ap Phillips, who was a strong supporter of both Henry IV and Henry V. The latter even visited St. Pierre. He used the occasion to hide his jewels in the tower of the building. The jewels were eventually found and passed on to Henry VI.

David ap Phillip's son preferred to be called Lewis and adopted this name as a family name. The Lewis family owned St. Pierre for several generations.

A lady in grey haunts St. Pierre with her occasional presence. The ghost has been described as a greyish shape that can be seen for a few moments. She likes to manifest in the doorway of a room referred to as 'The Sturges'.

The woman in grey is thought to be a member of the Lewis family. Legend has it that her ghost haunts St. Pierre because two suitors once fought a duel over her. The skirmish took place in a room called Maes Fawr which is now troubled by poltergeist activities.

The lady ghost is of a benevolent disposition. The first person to witness the haunting was a female guest who stayed at St Pierre near the end of the nineteenth century. Around the hour of breakfast she saw the Grey Lady in a corridor and automatically took her for the housekeeper. Later in the day she was surprised to learn that nobody had been in that part of the house around breakfast time.

Fred Hando, who researched the history of the houses of Gwent in depth, once stayed at St. Pierre and witnessed a haunting. He spent several nights in a small room in the top part of the building. When the room temperature dropped suddenly during the night Mr Hando awoke. He immediately felt a presence in the room. He believed that the presence was somehow trying to leave the room.

As seen in previous chapters, the root of a haunting often lies in a tragic event. Accordingly, the presence of spectres often creates an atmosphere of discomfort and sadness. However, one of the ghosts at St. Pierre seems to have a good time and thus proves that it is not always a dreary job to be a ghost. This particular ghost was once a gardener. The former gardener now haunts the garden of St. Pierre. He was named 'The Laughing Gardener' because he appears in the garden's gateway laughing heartily. Still laughing he walks through the garden and crosses the road. Thereafter he walks to the churchyard where he disappears.

Colwyn Bay (Bae Colwyn)
The projectionist of the Princess Theatre Bingo and Social Club

Unfortunately, there will always be sceptics that ridicule even the most reliable witness accounts of hauntings. However, the incident that occurred at the Princess Theatre Bingo and Social Club in Colwyn Bay makes it hard to deny the existence of the supernatural.

In 1990 Sandra Lloyd, a manageress, took a number of pictures in the club after closing time. She was rather surprised when she detected a ghostly figure floating over a barman on the developed pictures. The figure had not been there when the pictures were taken. These pictures were eventually published in the *County Pioneer*. This spectre has appeared to members of staff on numerous occasions. They described the ghost as a fleeting, hazy figure. Their description is identical with the spook captured on the pictures. The ghost seems to dislike crowds of people and thus manifests itself mostly after closing time.

The haunting most likely has its origins in the accidental death of a man. This incident goes back to the days when the building was still used as a cinema. It is said that a projectionist died in an accident in the projection box.

Several witnesses have also heard inexplicable noises in the club. It is quite conceivable that these strange noises are caused by the ghost on the picture.

Conwy
The unfortunate chambermaid of the Castle Hotel
The Castle Hotel in Conwy has a long history. Before it became a hotel the building was used as coaching inn. In even more remote times a Cistercian abbey occupied the site. A few of the hotel's former residents have stubbornly refused to go away.

A spectral blond girl of about twelve years of age often shows herself in the building. There is some historical evidence to support the appearance of the girl. A girl that fits the description was in the employ of the hotel in the 1920s. She worked as a chambermaid. The young girl fell ill but the manageress refused to allow her a period of rest and forced her to keep working. It is thought that the girl died as a result of the harsh treatment. Her last wish was to have her corpse sent back home to Anglesey. Instead of complying with the last wish of the girl the manageress had her buried in the adjacent graveyard. The girl's ghost returned from the tomb to haunt the hotel. Her body was finally transferred to Anglesey but the haunting did not stop. It continues to this present day. It is to be hoped that the phantom monk who also lives in the hotel is able and willing to offer the unfortunate chambermaid some spiritual comfort.

Most people like the consoling presence of a cat neatly curled up beside them on the bed. They enjoy the gentle rumbling purr and the occasional treadling of the paws. It is a different story altogether when the cat is a visitor from the world beyond. Like a cat of flesh and blood the phantom cat of the Castle Hotel still feels drawn to the warmth of a cosy bed. The phantasmal cat has been known to walk over beds during the night.

The cellar! Generally we do not wish to know what dark secrets a cellar might hold. We have no great desire to find out who or what dwells there. It sometimes does not even matter whether or not we wish to find out what lurks in a basement: whatever lives there seeks us out. One night an employee of the hotel who had work to do in the cellar was pushed aside against a wall by somebody or something. He felt that an invisible entity forced its way past him.

Corwen, Denbighshire
The Haunted Room of the Glyndŵr Hotel

The Glyndŵr Hotel offers a comfortable home to a spectral woman. Every day she probably enjoys three delicious spectral meals in the hotel's dining room. On another thought the building most likely has always had a link with haute cuisine. After all, the Glyndŵr in Corwen was once a monastery. The saying is that monks used to have a healthy appetite. There is nothing to be said against this. However, it seems that the monk involved in the legend of the Glyndŵr Hotel did not only look after his culinary well-being. He had other appetites apart from that, and it seems he broke one of his vows. It was probably a blessing too – or would have been if the two protagonists had not been up against a stern and unrelenting world. To cut a long story short, the monk fell in love with a beautiful woman. It must have been clear to the two lovers that ecclesiastical law did not allow such a relationship. When the liaison finally came to an end the woman died broken-hearted. Her ghost has returned to the place where she used to be so happy. She often shows herself in a particular bedroom. The room is therefore known as 'The Haunted Room'.

It is much to be hoped that the two unfortunate lovers will one day be together in another life.

Cwm, Denbighshire
Brother against brother at the Blue Lion Inn

The haunting of the Blue Lion Inn in Cwm has its origin in a conflict between two brothers, which had a fatal end.

It all goes back to the days when the inn was still a farmhouse. The farmer had two sons who disliked one another with a great passion. The brothers had frequent and often violent arguments. One day the villagers were surprised to learn from the farmer that one of his sons, John Henry by name, had left Cwm for good. Not long after this curious incident some workmen uncovered a mysterious grave in the nearby churchyard. The remains of a man were found on top of a coffin. The corpse was identified as John Henry, who had apparently been killed. He was probably murdered at the farmhouse and his corpse was hidden in another person's grave at night. The identity of the murderer has never been found out. The most likely candidate for the murder is John's brother.

The ghost of John Henry now appears at the inn and looks just as he had looked when he was alive. He is invariably dressed in the fashion of the period in which he was murdered, with a waistcoat and breeches. He always carries a heavy sack on his shoulders. The ghost also frequents the churchyard. Sometimes John Henry manifests himself together with two other ghosts, believed to be his father and brother.

There is no way of knowing whether John Henry is in any way linked with a supernatural event that sometimes occurs at the Blue Lion Inn. A former proprietor of the Inn, Mr

Evans, used to keep a few unusual pets behind the pub, a monkey, snakes and an alligator. When he checked on them one morning in 1969 he discovered that the cages had been opened during the night. The animals had used the opportunity to escape. Fortunately they had not gone far. Mr Evans found all of them and put them back in their cages. He was quite surprised when he was confronted with the same situation on the following morning. Once more somebody had opened all the cages during the night. Mr Evans believed that this was the doing of animal rights activists. In order to gather some evidence he sprinkled sand around the cages. He hoped to secure the footprints of the bothersome nocturnal visitors. In the morning Mr Evans found the cages open yet once again. Contrary to his expectation there were no footprints except for those the animals had made.

Sometimes a female ghost appears in the inn. The nature of this haunting differs considerably from most of the supernatural phenomena explored in this chapter. The ghost communicates with the witnesses! This particular lady ghost prefers to dress in blue and has been described as elderly. Her presence has been noticed on numerous occasions. Thus a cleaner once saw the lady in blue standing near the window of a dining room in the upstairs part of the house. The presence of the Blue Lady was inexplicable as the inn was closed to the public at that time of the day.

The young son of a former owner of the Blue Lion also had an encounter with the Blue Lady in his bedroom. She just entered the room and lay down on the other bed. The Blue Lady made an attempt to communicate. She told the young boy that she did not feel well.

Cydweli, Carmarthenshire
The hospitable ghosts of the Mason Arms
With its thatched roof, the Mason Arms in Cydweli certainly looks like a building with a long tradition. The pub is thought to be 700 years old, old enough to have picked up a few ghosts. It is believed that the Mason Arms is haunted by about a dozen ghosts. Most of them have not shown themselves in recent decades.

The spectral population of the pub is of a peaceful nature, as one particular incident proves. When a new landlady took over she found the chairs of the pub neatly arranged in a circle. She was amazed at the sight of the chairs because nobody had been in the building. The phantasmal legion of the pub had given her a friendly and cheerful welcome.

Deri, Gelli-gaer, Glamorgan
The guardian of the Bailey's Arms Hotel
Murder, romance, happiness, lies, greed etc. are causes that can lead to a haunting. The lady ghost of the Bailey's Arms Hotel in Deri has an entirely different reason to haunt her environment. She acts as a guardian and protector. She is therefore the benefactor of those to whom she appears.

On a Sunday afternoon in 2002 Caroline and her partner, together with the partner's brother and father, went to the Bailey's Arms. Caroline was then over five months pregnant, and therefore abstained from alcoholic drinks. The experience she had during that afternoon can therefore not be attributed to drunkenness.

Caroline was chatting with her partner's brother when of a sudden she began to suffer from a splitting headache. Around the same time Caroline noticed a lady in a long grey skirt and a close-fitting bodice approaching the table. The lady's hair was done up in a bun. Dressed in such an old-fashioned way the lady looked completely out of place. It seemed to Caroline that the lady in grey somehow conveyed a mental message to her. Caroline was sure that the lady had asked her if she and her baby were all right. As nobody else seemed to have taken notice of the lady in grey, Caroline attributed her appearance to the headache. She therefore went to the toilet to refresh herself. On her way back Caroline decided that the encounter with the strange lady was too realistic to have been caused by a simple headache. She mentioned the incident to her friends. Her partner's father readily believed her and made inquiries. The landlord informed him that the lady in grey had been seen on numerous occasions in the past, but that she had not been active for a while.

A few months later Caroline gave birth to a baby son whom she called Alun. Alun's birth was complicated. Yet Caroline always felt that neither she nor Alun had ever been in danger because she was certain that the phantom lady had been watching over them. Caroline believes the phantom lady has been keeping her son safe ever since.

Garden City, Flintshire
An ordinary ghost at the Queensferry Hotel?

The ghost of the Queensferry Hotel in Garden City is quite ordinary. Superficially studied, it cannot compete with impressive spectral entities like phantasmal monks or lady ghosts. Dressed in a humble dark trench coat, this male ghost seems to be only of mediocre quality. Yet one should not underestimate the phantom. The ghostly wearer of the trench coat often spreads an atmosphere of extreme dread. On one occasion the ghost scared a witness speechless.

Fred used to work and live at the hotel. He was also allowed to practised with his band in one of the cellar rooms after closing time. During the practice sessions Fred often rushed up to the kitchen to fetch refreshments for the band.

One night when Fred was in the kitchen he heard knocking sounds from the front door area. When he investigated the room he found it completely deserted. Over a period of time the phenomenon occurred several times.

Eventually, the band began to practise upstairs. The musicians soon became aware of phantom footsteps on the stairs and in some of the disused rooms upstairs. Fred explored those rooms, but they were completely empty.

Soon the haunting went into its next phase. One evening Fred locked up and switched on the burglar alarm. Then he retired to his room on the first floor together with his girlfriend Sharon. During the night the alarm went off. Fred raced down the stairs to check the ground floor rooms. As soon as he reached the taproom he saw an uncanny man dressed in a dark trench coat, boots and a hat. Fred chased upstairs again to awaken his cousin Wayne, who also had a room at the pub. Together they searched the building from attic to cellar but they found no trace of the intruder.

On the following day Fred informed the landlord about the incident. He learned that the landlord was well acquainted with the haunting.

Sheila, who now owns the pub, has heard a number of phantom noises, including barrels being shifted around in the cellar when nobody is anywhere near them, and false alarms. She and her family have also heard footsteps on the stairs. Sheila's daughter would often wake up in the middle of the night screaming with fear. The haunting scared her so much that she was unable to speak. Frightened into silence she would just point towards the corridor. Apparently the ghost was visible only to her.

Sheila also knows another witness who has seen the man in the trench coat. The witness was able to add another detail. Because of this witness account it is known that the hat the spectre wears is actually a fisherman's hat.

Hawarden (Penarlâg), Flintshire
She taps on a door in the Glynne Arms
The death of a child always seems to be particularly tragic. A young life is snuffed out like the flame of a candle. Years ago a young boy was fatally injured outside the Glynne Arms when a horse bolted on the street in front of the pub. He was carried through the pub's front door and died in the nearby corridor. The boy was about twelve years old when he died. His ghost can often be seen wandering around in the building.

The Glynne Arms is also reputed to be haunted by the ghost of a woman. She prefers to remain invisible. Nonetheless she has means and ways of making her presence known to the occupants of the building. Witnesses have frequently heard the sound of feminine footsteps on the stairs and along the corridor. The spectral woman always stops in front of a certain bedroom door and taps on it lightly. Her appearance is also connected with a strong scent of perfume.

Hay-on-Wye *(Y Gelli)*, Powys
The hound of the Baskerville Hall Hotel
Ghosts are almost always locally well-known. In a sense they acquire the status of local celebrities. A few lucky ones even climb up higher on the ladder of fame. They make their way into literature and become known all over the world. It is much to be deplored that none of these international phantasmal stars has ever been awarded an Oscar for good haunting.

The spooky stars of a haunting do not necessarily have to be human, as the following account shows. The ghost of the Baskerville Hall Hotel in Hay-on-Wye does certainly not belong to the homo sapiens group. Nevertheless the spectre is quite effective. It has gained world fame.

Baskerville Hall in Hay-on-Wye is the source of Arthur Conan Doyle's *The Hound of the Baskervilles*. The famous author relocated the legend of Baskerville to Cornwall in order to protect the anonymity of the people involved. In reality the dog-haunting is linked with the history of the Baskervilles and the Vaughans, who are their relatives. The Baskervilles frequently married members of the Vaughan family who lived in the vicinity of their estate. The Vaughans were once troubled by a horrible black dog. It is thus quite likely that the dog-haunting of Baskerville Hall goes back to the Vaughans.

However, there is also strong evidence to support the theory that the haunting of Baskerville Hall has its origin in an incident that took place on the estate long ago. According to this legend a past master of Baskerville Hall kept a big hound to protect the manor from wolves. One night the hound made out a wolf and barked and growled at it. The master awoke from his sleep, armed himself with a spear, and rushed out to see what the matter was. He failed to notice the wolf in the darkness and concluded that he owned a useless dog that had awakened him needlessly. Seething with anger, he stabbed the dog through the head with his spear. He realised too late that his loyal dog was right and that there really was a wolf near the house. The ghost of the murdered dog began to haunt the manor.

The unjust slaying of the hound of Baskerville Hall has to be taken with a pinch of salt. It may only be another version of the widely spread *Leitmotif* of the 'wronged dog'. As seen in the article on the Royal Goat Hotel in Beddgelert, Wales has another famous and unjustly killed dog. Somewhat farther afield, in Ireland, the young Sedanda killed Culann's hound. Unlike the haunting of the Royal Goat Hotel, which is almost certainly a fabrication, the ghost of the Baskervilles appears to be real and of great antiquity. The coat of arms of the Baskervilles strongly supports this theory. It is old and it shows the head of a canine pierced by a spear.

Be it as it may, the Hound of the Baskervilles cannot

complain about loneliness. There are plenty of human ghosts around to pat him on the head or give him a good rub behind the ears.

Visitors may sometimes bump into an elegant gentleman on the grand staircase. He seems to be real enough, but upon closer inspection one will find that he is a guest from the realm beyond. The elegant gentleman may sometimes come across the ghost of a man who has been seen walking on the balconies outside Rooms 3 to 7. There is probably romance in the air too. A lady in white has been seen wandering around in the garden. The theme of two men and a beautiful lady provides material for a Shakespearean tale of romance and tragedy.

Henllan, Denbighshire
A sea captain and his wife haunt the Llindir Inn
Unlike the Baskerville Hall Hotel, the Llindir Inn does not have a cute little phantasmal lap-dog with saliva-dripping teeth. If spooks were measured by the standards of the hound, the Llindir ghosts would probably be classified as boring. Nonetheless the haunting is somewhat unique. It is a romantic husband-and-wife-haunting, if romantic it can be called. The haunting certainly calls into question the marriage vow of 'till death us do part'. Sometimes this does not seem to happen. The readers must decide for themselves whether this is a blessing or not.

Llindir Inn in Henllan began its life in the thirteenth century as a hostelry. During its long history several tragic events occurred in the building. One of them has led to a haunting. The identity of the ghost of Llindir Inn is somewhat controversial. Some witnesses believe they have had an encounter with a female ghost whereas others maintain that the ghost is definitely male. Another solution can be put forward which is that two ghosts are involved in the haunting, husband and wife.

A sea captain and his wife, Sylvia, owned the inn about 300 years ago. The captain often sailed away for many months, too long for Sylvia. She took several lovers in his absence.

One day the captain returned unexpectedly. On his way to the inn he was caught in a storm. By the time he reached his home he was wet to the skin. The captain made straight for the bedchamber to change his clothes. When he entered the chamber he caught Sylvia red-handed with a lover. In a fit of anger he drew his dagger and killed Sylvia's paramour.

Sylvia threw herself at her husband's feet and begged forgiveness. The captain could not find it in his heart to forgive his wife. He strangled Sylvia with his own hands. Husband and wife now haunt the inn.

Sylvia's haunting is quite harmless. Her ghost has been described as pretty. She always wears a blue gown. If she finds a man sleeping alone in a bed in her former bedchamber she lies down right beside him. Some people are lucky indeed!

Contrary to his wife, the sea captain's ghost is of a violent disposition. The saying is that old habits die hard. This seem to be true in the case of the captain's ghost. A holidaymaker had an unpleasant encounter with the ghost of the captain. One night he was sleeping peacefully in his room when all of a sudden he felt hands closing around his throat. Somehow he managed to shake off the strangling hands but the ghost was not yet defeated. The invisible phantom pulled away the blankets, and noises of a struggle that was taking place somewhere in the room could be heard.

The nature of the witness statements strongly supports the theory that two ghosts are involved in the haunting. The two ghosts stick to their individual behavioural patterns. Sylvia had several lovers when she was alive. As a ghost Sylvia still behaves in much the same way: she tries to join male sleepers in bed when the opportunity presents itself. Her husband, the sea captain, was a violent man who thought nothing of strangling a man with his own hands. In recent times some witnesses have complained about being strangled by a phantom. It is therefore tempting to argue that the captain's ghost is behind these attacks.

And if they have not died they are still cheating, strangling and stabbing one another.

Holywell *(Treffynnon)*, Flintshire
The considerate ghost of the Talacre Arms

The Talacre Arms in Holywell lacks the romantic aspect of a husband-and-wife haunting. However, the ghost that visits this pub has a far more appealing character than either of the two cheating and murdering spectres of the Llindir Inn. Unlike the violent captain and his unfaithful wife, this ghost is able to love. The spectre shows great love for animals, which makes it an endearing entity from the ghostly realm. The ghost never shows itself. Its presence can only be detected by its actions. As the ghost cannot been seen some proprietors have doubted its existence. Contrary to this, many of the locals in Holywell believe that Talacre Arms is haunted. They know that two of the pub's clients, Selwyn Edwards and a friend, felt an invisible presence squeezing past them while they were standing at the bar. The locals know all about Selwyn's encounter with the ghost, and more on top of it.

The saying is that light bulbs mysteriously fall out of their sockets and remain lit, and that the piano often plays on its own accord. One of the landlords strongly denied the numerous stories concerning his pub. Yet even he had to admit that on one occasion a light bulb fell out of its socket and had to be replaced. The new bulb fell out too. Consequently, yet another light bulb was put in. The third replacement remained put. However, the bulb exploded after a short while.

Pets never feel at ease in the pub. A labrador was so frightened that it leapt through an open window to escape from the premises. Another dog yelped in terror and ran out on the road where it was killed by a car.

The ghost itself seems to like pets. A while ago the spectre placed a saucer packed with meat on the floor in an upstairs room. The supernatural aspect of the incident was that the room was locked and nobody had been in it for some time. Odder still was that the saucer did not belong to the household and that the origin of the meat remained unknown. It is thought that the meat was left for a cat.

Kenfig *(Cynffig)*, Bridgend
The phantom organ of the Prince of Wales Pub

A few decades back, in 1982, the landlord and his wife were about to finish cleaning the bar area after closing time when they heard organ music in an upstairs room. The landlord's first thought was that somebody was playing a joke on him, so he rushed upstairs as fast as his feet could carry him. When the landlord threw open the door of the room from which the music was coming he found it completely deserted. Thereafter he searched the whole house without any results. When the haunting repeated itself the landlord called in a team of researchers.

During the investigation the team sent a strong electric current through the walls while the pub was closed. A tape recorder was used to record any acoustic activities stirred up by the electric current. The researchers came up with a positive result. They recorded organ music, disembodied voices that spoke in a language nobody understood, and the ticking of a clock. It should be noted that there was no clock on the premises that could have caused such a sound.

The experiment of the researchers supports the theory that a haunting is nothing but some kind of magnetic recording in the building substance which is similar in nature to a video recording. It is believed that the spectral recording is re-played when favourable circumstances come together.

Little Haven, Pembrokeshire
Bit by bit he appears at the Castle Hotel

'An unnatural death,' concluded those who inspected the body found on the scene.

'It must be', echoed the sergeant.

Surely, it must be so: why else should her body have been found on a lonely beach? People just do not go to the beach and die; maybe she drowned.

Yes, maybe she drowned. All things being said this does not mean that she is not around anymore. Sometimes the world does not obey the rules of what is commonly viewed as logic. The lady whose corpse was found on the beach is still here in a phantasmal sort of way. We do not know whether death has left her somewhat pale around the nose because she appears at the hotel as an invisible spectre. But this does not imply that she is not there. She is most definitely with us. Sure enough we can hear her. The haunting concentrates on one of the bedrooms. The door of the room is opened and some invisible feet walk through the room. The tread of the feet causes the floorboards to creak, which in itself is a sign of a haunting because the boards are new and nailed-down. They should therefore emit no sound when somebody walks on them.

The ghost of a man dressed in modern clothes appears to both staff and visitors in a scary manner. Slowly, as if savouring it, he manifests himself feet first, and then the rest of the body.

Purr! Treadle and treadle again! That is the way of the cats, a purr and a treadle. They very well know that humans enjoy that. There is something comforting in a purr and a treadle. The cat of the Castle Hotel in Little Haven is well aware of the feline role as a comforter. The cat has laudable intentions. Unfortunately the considerate feline has not thought of the counterproductive effects of its charitable actions. It is fine when a cat hops on a bed and one can feel the soft fur of the cat, but what happens when your hand goes right through the cat? You have arrived at the correct conclusion. It is not an undernourished cat but a feline ghost. Purr! Treadle! All of a sudden the purring and treadling is not so welcome any more. Why? Is it because the cat of the Castle Hotel is somewhat spectral? Does that really matter? The cat seems to be happy enough, which cannot be said of a vast number of the cat's human contemporaries.

Llanarthne, Carmarthenshire
The disorderly ghost of the Emlyn Arms
Sceptics will find a million reasons to deny a haunting. The evidence for the haunting of the Talacre Arms is particularly vulnerable. Some doubters may even argue that Selwyn Edwards and his friend were not reliable witnesses. They had a brush with an invisible entity. Who believes such stories? Many critics would probably mockingly ask Selwyn how many pints he had consumed when he felt the ghost.

On the other hand there are inconvenient ghosts like the one who has made its home at the Emlyn Arms in Llanarthne. This spectre has the same modus operandi as the entity at the Talacre Arms; the spook remains invisible. However, in this case even critics will find it hard to doubt the veracity of the witness statement. The statement was made by a policeman!

Emlyn Arms, once called Emlyn Arms Inn, was built as a coaching inn in the mid 1700s, but the haunting only struck in the twentieth century.

The first one to notice the ghost of Emlyn Arms was a maidservant of thirteen years on 29 December 1909. She heard somebody knocking and went to answer the door only to realise that no one was there. At the same time a candlestick fell from a shelf in the hallway and flew through the air and almost hit her.

The main centre of the haunting was in the kitchen. An invisible force began to throw around kitchen utensils. It frightened the landlady, Mrs Meredith, so much that she screamed loudly. Her screams attracted the attention of one of her neighbours, a Mrs Jenkins. Accompanied by her niece, Mrs Jenkins went over to the pub to offer her help. When Mrs Jenkins saw objects sailing through the air in the building she decided to leave immediately. Nonetheless, Mrs Jenkins provided help of sorts. She called her husband, a police constable. Mr Jenkins arrived at 2.30 in the morning and found the inn still very much haunted. In the beginning he attributed the disturbances to the presence of a burglar, especially when he heard footsteps on the stairs and in the bedrooms. When he stormed up the staircase to explore the bedrooms, flying bottles attacked him. At that point he still believed that a burglar was behind the eerie occurrences and that he was hiding under a bed. The constable checked the area under the bed and found it completely deserted. While he was crawling around on the floor a heavy ornament fell from a nearby shelf and almost hit him. In the end Mr Jenkins was forced to admit that the commotion in the house was not due to human activity.

At 3.30 in the morning Mrs Meredith and her maid ran away from the house and spent the remainder of the night at a friend's house. To her great dismay the haunting was still active in the morning. The constable still nursed a faint hope that the strange happenings in the house were caused by an intruder. Consequently, he had the pub cordoned off. This measure proved to be ineffective as no one was trapped in the cordon. Mr Jenkins was finally forced to conclude that the building was haunted.

Llanddarrog, Carmarthenshire
Mr and Mrs Bale of the White Hart Inn

Have you ever watched a mystery film in which the director skilfully uses sound effects to increase the element of tension and suspense, footsteps that reverberate in long empty corridors and heavy eerie breathing? The good news is that you do not need a TV licence to experience this type of feeling. You can have it almost for free. It will only cost you the price of a drink at the White Hart Inn in Llanddarrog.

The inn was constructed during the medieval period and is thus one of the oldest inns in Wales. The building has picked up a few ghosts on its journey through the centuries.

The shades of Trevor and Marietta Bale often appear in the White Hart. As the shared surname implies, Marietta and Trevor were a married couple. This haunting can therefore be classified as another husband-and-wife-haunting. Unlike the vengeful captain of the Llindir Inn in Henllan and his unfaithful wife, Marietta and her spouse are friendly ghosts. Trevor was a regular at the pub. It is known that he suffered from a respiratory illness. His heavy breathing can still be heard in the pub.

Some ghosts seem to enjoy their spectral existence. The Laughing Gardener of the St. Pierre Golf and Country Club offers evidence to support this theory. Angus, a former barman of the inn, also belongs to this group of jolly ghosts. Even when Angus was still alive he was good-natured and joked and laughed most of the time. He seems to have had a good reputation, although he was a bit of a womaniser.

While Angus and the Bales are friendly spirits, the inn also has a ghost one would not like to meet in a dark hallway. His name is rumoured to be Arnold or J. R. Soam. Sometimes the surname is given as Soliman. Arnold wears dark clothes, a long coat, boots and a hat. Legend has it that he was a witch-hunter. The ghost carries a black book. Arnold is often seen filling his book with notes. It probably contains the names of his victims.

Arnold may sometimes bump into a gentleman who shares his love for dark clothes. Apart from a liking for dark garb the two ghosts have little in common. Unlike Arnold the unidentified gentleman in black has a pleasing personality.

Whether the ghost of the blacksmith that sometimes manifests in the bar room can be persuaded to have a pint with dear old Arnold at some point in the future remains an open question. It is much to be hoped that the inn also has its share of spectral mares. Otherwise the smith may get a mite bored. As long as he can shoe the odd ghost horse he will be fine.

There are several female ghosts at the White Hart. Arnold and the smith and the gentleman in black probably feel a little downhearted as the female ghosts do not seem to take any notice of them. Instead they love to gather in the television room. It appears that they prefer 'Coronation Street' to Arnold's company, which upon reflection may not be a bad choice. Unfortunately, this leaves the smith and the gentleman in black in a somewhat disadvantaged position. It has been suggested that they should refine their courting techniques. A spectral nosegay now and again may help.

Not all ghosts at the White Hart are human. The spectre of a dog that died towards the end of the twentieth century has been spotted walking around in the rooms. Although his name was Homer he should not be confused with the author of the *Iliad* and the *Odyssey*. Compared to the spectral pooch at the Baskerville Hall Hotel, Homer seems to be a mere trainee.

The White Hart also has a tiny museum section. In the main bar there is a shovel on display which was used as a murder weapon. The exact details of the murder have got lost in the mists of time.

Llandeilo, Carmarthenshire
What happened at the King's Head Hotel?
History has a way of forgetting the human element and leaves only the bare bones of an event. Names fade away and images become blurred. Who was the pretty red-head that haunts the King's Head Hotel in Llandeilo? What was her name? Was she happy? Did she laugh a lot? Did she have a favourite doll when she was little, or a purring cat that curled up beside her at night?

It is believed that the haunting of the King's Head Hotel goes back to the 1830s. In those years a beautiful red-haired woman fell from one of the hotel's windows and died as a result of the fall. The ghost fits the description of the woman who died in the accident. She especially haunts the area of the bar. Sometimes she does not show herself in her human shape but as a patch of yellowish vapour.

Did she really die in an accident? Did she maybe commit suicide? Was she maybe even murdered?

Llanelli, Carmarthenshire
A tragic love story at the Thomas Arms
The Thomas Arms in Llanelli was once the scene of the story of a forbidden love. It is not a story of an extramarital love affair, but rather one of a woman who meets another woman. In those days society was not ready to accept homosexual or lesbian love. It becomes especially complicated when there is also a male lover involved.

Petra was in love with another woman, Roberta, but at the same time she expected a child by the owner of the public house. It is known that the proprietor's name was Thomas and that he maltreated Petra. The exact circumstances of her death have never been found out. All that is known is that she fell down a flight of stairs. The fall killed her almost instantly. It is rumoured that Thomas may have pushed her down the stairs. Petra is probably happier in death than in life. Death has united her with her female lover. Petra and Roberta now haunt the building together.

The ghost of Michael Lewis, a deceased miner, sometimes visits the pub. He died in a mine that once existed under the Thomas Arms. In Michael's household there was a young girl whose name was Elizabeth. She was considered Michael's daughter. Only he knew that the girl was the fruit of a forbidden love, the fruit of incest. Elizabeth's real father was her mother's uncle. It is generally believed that the secret of Elizabeth's true identity compels Michael's ghost to haunt the pub which he must have frequented in his lifetime and under which he died.

There is always something mysterious about old cellars and true enough a dark secret lurks in the cellar rooms of the Thomas Arms. It is rumoured that the cellar was once used for black magic rituals that involved infant sacrifice. Stay there at night and if you are lucky (or should one say unlucky?) you will hear the disembodied voices of children, bloodcurdling and terrifying cries, and sobs.

Llanfihangel Crucornau, Monmouthshire
The phantom hangman of the Skirrid Mountain Inn

Who would like to have a drink under a gibbet or in a place where a gibbet once stood? Who would like to dine near a mortuary slab? All those in favour, hands up, please! Apparently, quite a number of people seem to be undeterred by such a suggestion.

The Skirrid Mountain Inn in Llanfihangel Crucornau is thought to be the oldest pub in Wales. Its existence can be traced back to 1110. A number of windows and beams and one of the doorways still consist of the original building material. For a large part of its history the Skirrid served as a court building and place of execution. From the twelfth to the seventeenth century almost 200 people were executed in the inn. The court met in a room on the first floor. Prisoners awaiting their trials were held in a small room halfway up the stairs. On their way to the court room they could catch a glimpse of a grisly beam across the staircase which served as gallows. The old beam still bears the marks of the hangman's rope. When the executioner had done his work the dead bodies were laid out on a slab of stone. The former mortuary slab has survived the passage of time. It has become part of the stairs.

The area where the hangings took place appears to be the most haunted part of the house. The ghost of a former hangman often shows himself on the stairs, sometimes in company of some of his victims. A number of customers who were unaware of the inn's past complained about a feeling of strangulation when they used the staircase. In some cases rope burns inexplicably appeared on their necks. Others felt dizzy on the stairs, and troubled by an imperceptible presence.

The ghost of a local celebrity, Judge Jeffries, sometimes manifests itself in the rooms on the upper floors. Judge Jeffries had a fearsome reputation, and was commonly known as 'the hanging judge'. The spectre of John Crowther can frequently be seen in the inn. He has probably returned to the Skirrid to settle accounts with the judge. Judge Jeffries sentenced John to death by hanging for stealing sheep. John Crowther's ghost is active all over the building.

Not all spectral occupants of the inn are as unpleasant as Judge Jeffries. The ghost of Father Henry Vaughn, a priest from a local church, has been described as friendly. His presence is thought to spread a benevolent atmosphere.

One of the former proprietors feels apparently drawn back to the inn. Fanny Price, whose husband owned the Skirrid during the mid nineteenth century, takes part in the haunting. In 1873, barely thirty-five years old, she died of tuberculosis.

Fanny's preferred location is Room 3.

The Skirrid Mountain Inn also hosts a lady in white. She often walks around in the rooms of the inn. It is thought that her presence leaves behind a beautiful smell of perfume. More experienced ghosts would presumably argue that the lady is not so well-versed in the art of spooking. Every ghost with a few years of work experience knows that a pungent corpse smell is more effective. Add a rattling chain and you are almost there. And hey presto, if you have mastered the art of carrying your head under your arm nobody will ever argue with you. Oh dear, the poor lady still has to do a little bit of studying. Be it as it may, even the most unrelenting spectral critics see themselves forced to admit that the lady in white does exceedingly well on the sound effects. She always ensures that the rustling of her dress is clearly audible. Upon reflection she should maybe train in ghostly breathing.

At times the haunting can be quite harmful. In some of the rooms the guests experience aches and pains and a feeling of oppression on the chest.

After a brush with the grim Judge or the spectral soldiers that sometimes appear in the courtyard, one will possibly think nothing of the ghostly laughter, slamming of doors and a variety of similar noises that sometimes haunt the premises.

Maesteg, Bridgend
In Room Five at the Castle Public House

Murder always wants out. There will always be somebody to point an accusing finger at the murderer and even if it is only a ghost. The incident at the Castle Public House in Maesteg is indeed one of murder.

Who can say what exactly happened so many years ago in the room now known as Room 5? It is rumoured that a former landlady was murdered in that room. Tempers flared and a violent deed was committed. Maybe the murderer was driven by greed? Or was it even a crime of jealousy and passion? Too many years have passed to establish the exact motive of the murderer. It is commonly believed that the villain was the landlady's own husband. Be it as it may, the crime was committed, but apparently the criminal has not quite gotten rid of his victim. The landlady is still there. She often returns to the scene of the crime, room 5. Quite in keeping with supernatural research Room 5 seems to be colder than the rest of the house. Now and again the deceased landlady leaves Room 5 to visit the staircase. The phantom can then be seen walking downstairs. She usually vanishes after a short while.

Marford, Wrexham
The violent ghost of the Trevor Arms Hotel
The ghost of the Trevor Arms Hotel is not quite as violent as the sea captain at the Llindir Inn. Nonetheless those who have had dealings with the phantom have a story to to tell.

The Trevor Arms looks back on a long history. It began its life in the seventeenth century when it was a coaching inn. Some of the inn's former occupants and clients now haunt the building. Sometimes they get carried away a bit and become a mite too personal. One of them has even quite a temper. This unidentified ghost is said to have attacked a number of guests in Room 7 and Room 10. Several lodgers have complained about being pushed down on their beds by an invisible force during the night. Sometimes the spectre just sits down on the bed. A witness who often stays at the hotel has described this occurrence in great detail. On one occasion he woke up well after midnight because he could feel a presence sitting on his bed.

While ghosts have been seen all over the building, the main haunting appears to be focused on the bedrooms. Both staff and lodgers have experienced the haunting in the bedrooms.

There may be a connection between the supernatural phenomena in the bedrooms and the ghostly lady who has been seen wandering around in the hotel. Well after closing time, when nobody should have been in the area, a cleaner was surprised to see an old woman wandering around on the ground floor. After a while the old lady vanished before her eyes.

Even the area around the hotel is haunted. A phantom man wearing a hat haunts the archway between the outbuildings.

Mold, Flintshire
The pipe smoker of the Boar's Head
The ghost of the Boar's Head definitely defies the smoking ban in public places. As shall be seen despite the law that has been passed recently in the UK the spectre continues to smoke on the premises of the pub.

There are controversial reports as to the appearance of the ghost. Sometimes it manifests itself in the tap room as a hazy mass roughly shaped like a human being. The hazy figure feels drawn to the area of the now bricked-up lounge door. From there the phantom makes its way in the direction of the living quarters where it vanishes into thin air. Some witnesses believe that the ghost is more than a hazy contour in the air. One of the patrons knows for sure that the ghost is male. He once had a brush with it and was able to make out the shape of a man in the misty apparition. The ghost was eventually named George.

When alive George seems to have been a passionate pipe smoker. Even now the spectral noises of a pipe being emptied into the fireplace can sometimes be heard. George must have loved the area around the fireplace. He now haunts his former cosy corner with a strong smell of tobacco and gin, and this despite the smoking ban.

George was most likely a former occupant of the building. The fact that he has been seen walking to the living quarters of the pub lends some substance to this theory. After a pleasant evening of smoking and drinking the ghost of George returns to his home just as George must have done when he was still alive. George died years ago but he has never left the Boar's Head in Mold.

Monknash *(Yr As Fawr)*, Vale of Glamorgan
The mortuary room at the Plough and Harrow
The history of this pub in Monknash goes back to 1383. As its English name implies, Monknash had a connection with monastic life. It used to be the farm of a monastery of a Cistercian abbey based in Neath. But it also has a touch of piracy and Treasure Island about it.

The taproom of the Plough and Harrow is large, but centuries ago its architecture was quite different. There used to be a sinister chamber at the far end of the modern taproom, whose walls have been knocked down to enlarge the business area. The former chamber has a blood-chilling history. It was used to store the bodies of the victims of a band of beach pirates who were known as the Wreckers of Wick. The pirates would mislead ships by hanging lanterns on sheep and allowing them to wander along the cliffs. Thus deceived, the crews of many incoming ships believed they were approaching the docks of Cardiff or Barry. In reality they were directly heading for the dangerous Nash sandbank, where the ships often ran aground and shattered. The corpses of the casualties were stored in the chamber that once existed in the taproom of the modern pub until the carpenters had produced enough coffins to bury them.

The ghosts of some former victims still linger at the inn. They like to move around glasses and chairs. Opinions are divided as to whether the ghosts are dangerous. Some former landlords were not quite convinced of the ghosts' harmlessness.

Monmouth *(Trefynwy)*
The Cavalier of the Queen's Head Hotel

Shakespeare once wrote in one of his plays that violent desires have violent ends. The incident that took place at the Queen's Head in Monmouth centuries ago is indeed a tale of violence and murder.

A Cavalier had a plan and the more he thought about it the better it seemed to him. It was common knowledge that his hated enemy, Cromwell, often stayed overnight at the Queen's Head. He was going to make good use of this precious bit of knowledge. It was easy enough to find out the date of Cromwell's next stay at the inn. And now the day of the great event had finally come; Cromwell was on his way.

The Cavalier sat at a table in a dimly lit corner of the Queen's Head. He had not drunk much while he was waiting for his enemy, just a mug of ale. He needed a steady hand for what he had in mind. The Cavalier contemplated ordering another one. It would arouse suspicion if he didn't. He knew he had to go easy on his next drink. He couldn't afford to be drunk. What was keeping Cromwell so long?

Cromwell arrived when the Cavalier was half-way through his second drink. The Cavalier glanced furtively across the taproom to where Cromwell sat with his retainers. He was in a pensive mood. From the distance Cromwell seemed to be quite a likeable man, a man like you and me. He even laughed occasionally. Imagine that: Cromwell laughed. As the evening passed he found himself quite liking the man, but that would never do: Cromwell was the enemy and that was that. The Cavalier yawned. He could hardly keep his eyes open. It had been a long day and a long journey. Travelling to the Queen's Head had taken him some time and that damned man

Cromwell never seemed to get tired. Was that the secret of Cromwell's success, a sheer endless supply of strength? Once he had dealt with Cromwell he wouldn't be so strong anymore. He would see to that all right. But when would this chap actually rise and retire to his chamber?

Cromwell did eventually rise to his feet and made his way to his bed-chamber, although it took the Cavalier another mug of ale to see this moment arrive. Cromwell said his goodbyes for the night and a few moments later the darkness of the stairway that led to his bed-chamber swallowed him. Unnoticed, the Cavalier tiptoed after his enemy. He was sweating profusely now and his hands were shaking. It was harder than he thought. Everything seemed so easy just a short while ago. He had to get it done and over with before he lost his nerve. He paused for a few moments in the darkness of the stairwell. Cromwell's footfall made the wooden floorboards creak above him in the corridor. A door opened and closed. That was it then. Cromwell was in his room. Silent like a shadow the Cavalier rushed upstairs and reached the door of Cromwell's bed-chamber. He put his ear against it and made out that his enemy was getting ready for bed. The Cavalier knew that he should give his victim time enough to settle in bed, but what if somebody came along right now? That would never do. A film of sweat glistened on his forehead and the palms of his hands were wet. Of a sudden he felt cold too. He swallowed hard. Yes, this was the moment. He could not afford to wait any longer. Somebody was bound to come along, he was sure.

He breathed deeply to steady himself but his hand was still shaking when he drew his loaded pistol and kicked open the door of the bed-chamber. In the light of a candle he saw the shock in the face of his enemy. This was a man who had laughed in the taproom an hour or so ago. Then Cromwell seemed happy and relaxed. How could he take that wretch's life now? But it had to be done. His pistol-hand stabbed forward and he ripped back the trigger. All wrong, he thought. He knew it the moment he pulled back the trigger so hastily. That's not the way it is done. That threw the pistol off target. The Cavalier swore loudly as the flint ignited the gunpowder in the barrel and the shot rang through the silence of the night. In a split-second the acrid smell of gunpowder hung densely in the air. With a leaden thud the bullet hit the rafters. Cromwell was unharmed and already on his feet reaching for his sword and shouting for attention. There was simply no time to reload the pistol. The Cavalier threw away the useless firearm and drew his dagger. When he heard the tramping of booted feet and a cacophony of voices he instantly knew that Cromwell's henchmen were already after him. He turned on his heels and began to run for his life. The odds were very much against him. How in the devil's name was he going to get out of that inn? Sure enough his enemies soon blocked his way and had him surrounded. The ensuing melée was brief and had a predestined end. Bleeding from several wounds the Cavalier sank to the ground. So that's what it is like, he thought philosophically, despite the pain. That's what it is like when one dies. Then everything went dark around him.

The Cavalier is back at the hotel in all his glory. And what is more, he looks almost as good as new: maybe a bit transparent, but that is nothing to be worried about. This is the way it is with ghosts. The spectre still feels attracted to the Lord-Protector's former bedroom. This room is the centre of the haunting. Old habits die hard.

The ghost of one of Cromwell's soldiers lurks in the corridors of the hotel. It is quite possible that there is a link between the phantom soldier and the Cavalier. Was he the man who killed the audacious would-be assassin? Will the Cavalier get even with the spectral soldier at some point in the future?

Neath *(Nedd)*
The cellar of the Greyhound Public House

Why should darkness be so different from light? After all, darkness is just the opposite of light. But yet darkness does not sit comfortably with human imagination. Human vision is so poor. It's easier for cats, isn't it? As long as there is a ray of light cats have well-nigh perfect vision. Owls feel quite comfortable in the darkness too. It is different with humans. Too much thinking seems to get in the way. What is, and what would be, or could have been, always frightens us. Oh yes, and there is the darkness of the night or a cave or a cellar. A cellar is like a cave, isn't it? Who can tell what dangers lurk in a cave? And for that matter, what dangers, if any, lurk in the cellar of the Greyhound in Neath? What is a cellar after all? It is a bit like a flat that has not been done up, for it is not worth your while as it is only meant to hold old junk. It holds barrels of beer and suchlike. Nothing more – and yet … what else is there in the darkness? *Who* else? Something is there all right, but what? If there weren't anything why would one feel so frightened? Why would one feel like running for one's life?

Is it just imagination that makes those who venture into the cellar part of the Greyhound feel uncomfortable? Many people have gone down into the darkness of the cellar of the Greyhound and felt the presence of something one would rather not like to meet. Doom! Danger! Death? Or worse? But yes, what lurks in the blackness of the Greyhound's cellar?

Sure, up to round about the year 2000 the Greyhound was a peaceful place. But then! We do not want to go into details about the cellar and all. There is just something there, you know. But there we go again. Let us rather talk about Bryn. We know more about Bryn. All right, Bryn was a former patron of the Greyhound. Bryn liked a mug of ale, so he did. But most of all he liked the Greyhound. Till death parts you, one should think. Hmm? You know, this is not always true.

Why else should Bryn be back at the Greyhound? And him dead as a doorknob, as one would say in Ireland. Bryn is dead all right ... but he is still there. He is quite harmless too. So why not have a drink with him? He definitely makes much better company than the captain at the Llindir Inn.

Pembroke, Pembrokeshire
Scent of lavender at the Port Hotel
The ghost of a former serving woman haunts the Port Hotel in Pembroke. The haunting appears to be of a relatively recent date as it was only noted from the 1940s onwards. Few facts about the woman's life have survived.

Yet, one endearing little detail is known. She must have loved lavender when she was alive. Her liking for lavender was not eradicated by death. Even now the scent of lavender announces her presence.

Pontargothi, Carmarthen
The thief of the Salutation Inn
The Salutation Inn in Pontargothi was once called Penrheol Inn. The inn was built over 600 years ago. A substantial part of the original building substance has survived. There are still plenty of old beams, flagstones and thick walls. The inn and its environment has a violent past. Numerous battles were fought around the inn and it is known that it sometimes served as an improvised field hospital. It is hardly surprising to learn that some of the combatants who died in agony should have come back from the realm of the dead.

One of them is Prince Llywelyn. Fighting seems to be a thirsty affair. A pint of ale is needed to quench a man's thirst. Accordingly, the ghost of the prince can sometimes be seen near the stable from where he makes his way to the taproom.

The spectres of some former owners still linger at the inn. One of them is the ghost of June. It is thought that she and her husband haunt the upper floor. June was hardworking and diligent, and under her guidance the inn became a prosperous business. Unfortunately, the same cannot be said of her husband. He was given to drinking and was also a thief. He squandered the money June earned, and needed still more. Thus one day he stole a box of pearls from June. This incident seems to have upset her beyond measure, so much indeed that she returned as a ghost after her death in 1874. The saying is that her ghost is searching for the pearls.

Lorna is another former landlady of the inn. She owned the inn a century prior to June's sad story. Lorna possessed great wealth. She therefore never needed to get personally involved in the running of the inn. She died in the middle of the eighteenth century. It is not known why she was buried in the cellar of the building. Legend has it that Lorna's husband also haunts the inn. He watches over his wife's tomb. The saying is that the ghost tries to prevent people from walking over Lorna's grave.

Henry Selwy and his partner Sam once owned the Salutation Inn. They seem to have liked the building so much that they have returned as ghosts. Sam's ghost is a bit mischievous. She makes her presence felt by moving objects around.

Five former ostlers and a stable boy, Daniel Davies, sometimes show themselves in the inn. The ostlers died in a fire that ravaged the inn. Daniel's death was only indirectly caused by the fire. He was kicked to death by a horse that was frightened by the conflagration.

Pontyclun, Rhondda Cynon Taf
Midnight at the Miskin Manor Hotel
While it is undoubtedly useful to view a haunting critically and with a good sense of humour the Miskin Manor Hotel in Pontyclun does indeed have a traditional ghost. The spectre

seems to be a firm believer in the twelve o'clock rule. The twelfth stroke of the clock means that it is midnight. Any reasonable ghost knows then that the time to spook has arrived. Punctuality is one of the foremost attributes of the ghostly lady that haunts the Miskin Manor Hotel. In classic ghost fashion she manifests herself quite regularly at midnight. She has been described as a nebulous figure that moves about somewhat and eventually dissipates.

The hotel is also home to the ghost of a little girl. She often plays in the garden and sometimes haunts one of the bedrooms. The saying is that the young girl died in a fire long ago.

The most troubled part of the house is the Oak Room, where the ghost of a former lord of the manor appears frequently. In addition there are ten spectres that can often be seen gathered around a table in the Oak Room. Listen now, you have lost your way. King Arthur's round table is thought to be more in the direction of Caernarfon.

A phantom gentleman in black sometimes shows himself in one of the rooms of the hotel where he can be seen looking out a window observing the lawn below.

Even the garden of the manor is haunted. A former gardener seems to have loved his work so much that his ghost frequently returns to his workplace.

Are we dead or alive? Is life but a dream and the living are dead in reality? The ghost who appeared to a client of the hotel one night seems to reason along those lines. This visitor had a frightening experience in one of the bedrooms. He was still awake in his bed which faced the bathroom. The man was astounded when somebody came out of the bathroom. The ghostly figure went to his bed and began to speak to the man telling him that he should not worry about anything anymore because he was dead! Then the ghost returned to the bathroom. The man was not quite sure whether the incident had really occurred because it was so unrealistic and unlike anything he had seen before. He dismissed the incident, thinking that contrary to his better knowledge he had fallen asleep and had had a dream. When he went to the bathroom he learnt that he had a true encounter with a ghost. The bathroom was littered with tissue paper: only the uncanny visitor could have littered the room.

Pontypridd, Rhondda Cynon Taf
The Victorian woman of the Maltsters Arms
Unimaginable dangers may lurk underground. It is the realm of the unseen. Who can tell what goes on in this dark cavity? The earth has spawned all sorts of likely and unlikely creatures over the millennia. Some of them are quite unpleasant, like the nightmarish being that haunts the cellar of the Greyhound as seen in a previous article. It is comforting to know that the cellar-haunting of the Maltsters Arms in Pontypridd is of a harmless nature.

The Maltsters Arms is a spacious building. Two levels and the Cellar Bar are open to the public. The latter is so called because it is located in the cellar. The employees of the pub avoid the Cellar Bar because it is thought to be haunted.

Jane is a member of staff who lives in the building. In February 2006 she cleaned up the pub after closing time. Her work took her to the Cellar Bar, where she had an encounter with a ghost. The incident took place around 4 o'clock in the morning. A female ghost no taller than 5ft 5in appeared near the fireplace in the cellar. She was in her mid twenties and had long dark hair. The spectre wore a long dress of the Victorian period. The phantasmal woman turned round and walked into the passage that leads to the toilets, where she disappeared.

It is known that the pub has a link with the Victorian era. In those days the building was used as a hotel. The ghost is believed to be a former lodger of the hotel.

Rhymney *(Rhymni)*, Caerffili
Murder at the Rhymney House Hotel?

Who hid the corpse and why? This is most definitely a case for Sherlock Holmes. In less than a minute he would tell us why the corpse of a maidservant was hidden in a well, a place so substantially far away from where she actually died in mysterious circumstances at Rhymney House several decades ago.

Rhymney House was built around 1801 as a home for the manager of the Rhymney Iron Company, whose owner was Richard Crawshay of Cyfarthfa in Merthyr Tydful. The building has since then changed owners many times and is now a hotel.

Richard Crawshay is associated with a mysterious incident that took place at Rhymney House. Legend has it that a maidservant had a liaison with Richard Crawshay and became pregnant by him. The affair distressed the young woman so much that she hurled herself out of the window of her bedroom, which was located on the topmost floor. It has been established without doubt that the young woman fell to her death from exactly that window. However, it has never been sufficiently explained why her body was found in the well behind the building. The maidservant's room was in the front part of the house, whereas the well was around the corner in the back of the house. How did the body get in the well? Who had cause to hide the body of the unfortunate woman? Surely this must have been murder. The ghost of the unfortunate maidservant is said to haunt Rhymney House.

Maybe the phantasmal man on horseback who has been seen on the road just outside the building witnessed the incident. If asked, could he tell us what happened on that fateful day? And what about the spectral teamster who often appears on the road near the hotel with his cart and horses? Did he happen to pass by when the maidservant died? Could he tell us anything? And then there is always the shade of a friendly lady who wears a long dress and a lace cap. Would she make a good witness? Probably not. Her mind seems to be too much on her work. Her love for children reveals that she must have been a nursemaid when she was alive. A former proprietor of the hotel even commented that the ghostly woman in the lace cap would 'tuck' his young daughter into bed at bedtime. Did the spectre of the elderly lady who sometimes appears in the back bar know the maidservant with the lace cap? The elderly lady likes a cosy evening at home. Watching the fire in the back bar seems to give her the greatest pleasure. The phantasmal girl that often stands in a corner of the back bar must have seen the elderly lady many times.

There is also a bit of a mystery. Why does the male ghost who has been spotted in the function room constantly watch the back bar from his lookout position? Is it just boredom? Or does the phantom expect to see something or somebody very specific – the murderer of the maidservant, perhaps?

Some ghosts are a bit impatient. A phantasmal man with a high hat sometimes appears in the corridor outside the kitchen. Once there he wastes no time and makes straight for the bar room where he has his night-cap. Maybe he is really desperate for a drink. The man's behaviour probably amazes the shade of the young boy who haunts the kitchen area.

Toilet ghosts seem to be quite fashionable these days. As seen in previous articles several inns are plagued by a toilet-haunting. It seems that the Rhymney House Hotel has jumped on the bandwagon. The Rhymney toilet ghost is by no means as scary as the one at the Rummer. However, upon reflection the spectre is not doing too badly. Within his limits this male ghost gives his all to do the good work. But sadly he has not yet quite learnt the technique of ghostly breathing. It is more of a cough. Users of the gents' toilet have often noticed the spectral coughing of a man in the toilet facilities. The uncanny noise is undoubtedly linked with the blackish ghost that has been seen entering the toilets on a number of occasion.

Although the rooms were instantly searched nobody has ever been found in them.

The male phantom who has been nicknamed 'The Guardian' has not yet been promoted to the illustrious rank of a toilet ghost. The best he can come up with is to stand near the ladies' toilets, where he makes a nuisance of himself by trying to prevent both staff and clients from using the stairs. This unusual behaviour is also the source of his nickname.

A family of ghosts assembles with regular frequency on the landing of the top floor. This family of five consists of a man, a woman, a young girl and two even younger children. The male ghost has been described as extremely dominant. The saying is that the child ghosts are afraid of him.

Another male shade haunts the laundry room. His presence seems to affect the CCTV cameras in this part of the building. They often fail and so far the engineers have not been able to find a reasonable explanation why this should be so.

Ghosts have also been sighted in Rooms 3 and 6. Room 3 is probably the most haunted area of the house. A child of around ten years of age who once stayed in Room 3 saw numerous people passing through the walls. They were elegantly dressed in suits and high hats. A male phantom sometimes appears in Room 6, where disembodied voices have also been heard.

This lively coming and going is thought to be due to some kind of opening between the worlds which allows the ghostly visitors to travel freely from one world to another. The exact centre of this rift between the dimensions is located in the area of Room 5 and the middle landing.

Needless to say that this veritable army of ghosts generates a lot of noise. A multitude of spectral sounds like rapping, rattling, slamming of doors, voices and so forth occurs in practically all parts of the house.

Rossett *(Yr Orsedd)*, Wrexham
The gibbet of the Golden Lion

Sometimes it is enough to possess an object that has a link with a tragic event to attract a haunting. When an old beam of wood was incorporated in one of the buildings of the Golden Lion in Rossett during some building or restoration work nobody ever thought that there was an extra price to be paid. It is all right to purchase a bit of cheap recycled wood, but one also has to be aware of its origin.

A man who was locally known as Jeffrey grievously injured a farmhand in the vicinity of Gresford. The farmhand survived the attack and witnessed against Jeffrey, who was found guilty of the crime and executed at Ruthin. His remains were transferred to Rossett and publicly displayed on a gallows. The body was eventually taken down and buried in an unconsecrated grave, which caused him to haunt the village.

The gibbet has survived the passage of time. Its wood was used as timberwork in an outbuilding of one of the village's inns, the Golden Lion. It is probably because of the presence of the bits and pieces of the gibbet that Jeffrey's ghost began to haunt the pub. His spectre sometimes appears in Room 2. Jeffrey is dressed in the working clothes of a ploughman. He has also been sighted on the landing in front of Room 2.

Swansea *(Abertawe)*
The phantom child of the Pontardawe Inn

The Pontardawe Inn in Pontardawe (now part of Swansea) is locally known as Y Gwachel ('the brothel', 'the coven', or as the Inn's website suggests, 'the hiding-place of scoundrels'). The present building stands on the remains of a much older alehouse. The old alehouse catered for the drovers that came down the nearby drover's road.

The owners, Huw and Siân, believe that their inn is haunted. One evening after closing time Huw sat in his office in the inn's cellar counting the day's income. Of a sudden he became aware of a presence in the room and looked up from the desk. Huw caught sight of a diminutive white shape which was about the height of a small child. The whitish figure made straight for the desk at which he was working and walked through it. The ghost continued on its route and disappeared through a wall.

The spectres love to play around with the inn's equipment. Glasses mysteriously fall from the top shelf without shattering on the stone floor. Sometimes the beer barrels in the cellar get shifted around, even if there is nobody around and all doors and hatches are locked and bolted.

Swansea
The shouting ghost of the Castellamare Restaurant
Modern buildings are not safe from ghosts. Two managers of the Castellamare Restaurant in Swansea learned that ghosts make no exceptions. They also strike in relatively new buildings.

Castellamare is a modern building near Bracelet Bay in the beautiful area of Mumbles in Swansea. The restaurant's toilets are haunted.

Once, well after closing time, the manageress who was still in the building heard somebody shouting in the men's toilet. Her first thought was that a customer had been accidentally locked in the toilet. Accordingly, she went to the rescue of the customer. To her great surprise there was nobody in the toilet. This was not a unique incident. The haunting continued. The ghost of an unidentified woman entered the toilets not too long after the first incident.

The spectres are not always harmless. Another manager was hit in the face by an invisible entity.

The ghost may not necessarily be connected with the actual building. A possible explanation for the haunting would be that the restaurant was built on naturally haunted ground. The haunting may thus go back to an incident in the remote past of the area. Violence must have occurred in the region as it was infested with smugglers. The ghosts that trouble the Castellamare could easily be smugglers who died a violent death or a victim of the smugglers – or maybe even both.

Tenby *(Dinbych-y-pysgod)*, Pembrokeshire
The Gypsy Lady of the Normandie Inn

What was life in a castle like? The inhabitants would have heard sounds that are totally unfamiliar to the sense of hearing of modern man. There would have been the rattling of the drawbridge when it was lowered and the creaking of heavy wagons passing over it. There would have been the screeching noise of the portcullis when it was either lowered or drawn up. The heavy footfall of the guards on the battlements would have been clearly audible to everyone, and so on. One would think that these sounds have fallen silent and can no longer be heard. This is not strictly speaking true. Sometimes they come to life again in the Normandie Inn in Tenby.

This may be because some of the walls of the old castle and bits of the castle's courtyard survive as parts of the Normandie Inn. The sound of phantom horses haunts the inn, the clattering of hooves in a courtyard that disappeared long ago.

The ghostly horses have spectral human company. Clients have complained about being prodded in the back by some invisible person. Was this invisible entity the ghost of the tall gentleman who sometimes manifests in the inn? He pays much attention to his appearance and wears fine clothes. Even inside the inn the man still wears his hat. Did he know the three elegantly-dressed gentlemen who frequently appear in a recess beside the fireplace when he was alive?

The most interesting ghost of the many that haunt the inn

is the spectre of a young woman. It is known that she was a serving girl at the inn. There is an atmosphere of mystery about the young woman. She is dressed in the fashion of the gypsies. Was she a Romany?

Tintern *(Tyndyrn)*, Monmouthshire
The Grieving Lady of the Anchor Inn

Sometimes the sound of cheerful music can be heard in the Anchor Inn. Normally there is nothing unusual about a musician performing in a pub. However, the Anchor Inn in Tintern does not quite fit the norm. The inn provides a venue for a musical ghost, who plays jolly tunes on his tin whistle.

Both staff and clients claim to have seen a White Lady roaming through the rooms of the inn. She is quite different from the merry musician. No joyful sound ever comes from her lips. The White Lady is full of sorrow. It is known that the White Lady's son went missing when she was alive. Distraught and overcome with grief she began to haunt the inn after her death. She now wanders through the Anchor searching for her missing child.

Usk *(Brynbuga)*, Monmouthshire
Who Haunts the Cross Keys Hotel?

Time is a great leveller. It makes uneven even. Lady Time forces even the mightiest man in the world to fall on his knees in front of her to beg for mercy when the hour of death arrives. Time is a great healer and a blessed giver of oblivion. However, sometimes one wishes that time did not wipe out so many details. Oblivion can be misleading to the point that some researchers are not sure whether the ghost that haunts the Cross Keys Hotel in Usk is male or female. Nonetheless they all agree that the Cross Keys is haunted. The crucial question is, who causes the haunting?

Some investigators believe that the ghost is that of a

monk; others are convinced that it is the ghost of a former serving girl.

On various occasions a spectre dressed in a long robe or gown has been seen in Room 3. This ghost also wanders around in one of the bedrooms on the upper floor. Apparently the ghost does not have what one would call a vivid imagination and only plays around a little with the latch of the door of Room 3. Yes, the latch of this door has been seen moving on its own accord here and there. Admittedly this can be somewhat disturbing at times. It could easily be a monk – it does wear a long robe, after all.

The history of the Cross Keys Hotel certainly seems to favour the monk theory. It is known that the inn was a hospice in the eleventh century. The building was then joined with nearby Usk Priory by means of a subterranean passage. Local history also teaches that a priest or monk was hung, drawn and quartered near the inn. The cruel manner of death could well have made the spirit of the cleric restless. Although one should have thought that the monk was quite dead after the treatment he received. So it is most definitely a spectral monk that haunts the hotel.

But hang on a minute, what about the maidservant? She committed suicide and it happened at the Cross Keys Hotel too all these many years ago. In those days they did not put your body in consecrated soil when you committed suicide. While some people did not care one bit others felt quite upset when this happened, upset enough to start a haunting. The spectre is said to wear a long robe – but does this necessarily imply that it is a monk's habit? The spooky character could well be a woman in a dress.

Oh dear, it is obvious: there are *two* ghosts, a monk and a maidservant. Let's give both of them some credit – they are doing reasonably good work. It is just a pity that so little is known about the fate of the maidservant. What drove her to such a desperate deed? Who was she really? Where did she laugh and run and play when she was a little girl? Who wept for her, if anybody, when she was dead? Let us hope that somebody shed some tears over her corpse.

Wrexham *(Wrecsam)*
An unsuccessful exorcism at the Thirsty Scholar
The owner of the Thirsty Scholar in Wrexham believes that her pub is haunted.

Around opening time she can usually feel the presence of several ghosts. Sometimes the ghosts can even be clearly seen. Heather May, a bartender, saw the shade of a man dressed in black near the patio. Even when the ghosts remain invisible they make their presence known vigorously. They send objects flying through the air. The phantoms throw around with crisps, ladles and beermats. They also open and shut doors and break glasses in the hands of the customers.

The haunting may be due to the pub's distressing past. The saying is that the building was once used as a mortuary. This may easily account for the haunting.

In 2005 the owner decided that enough was enough and called in a priest to give the pub a blessing. The priest was only moderately successful. The ghosts are still there but they are less active now.

Well, may be the ghosts have just taken some time off after centuries of intensive spooking.

2

Castles and their ghosts

Wales has often been described as the land of castles. From the green valleys of the eastern and southern borderlands to the mountainous regions of northern and western Wales the picturesque silhouettes of castles dominate the skyline. Both the residents and visitors alike are familiar with the names of the castles of Caernarfon and Harlech, Cydweli and Pembroke, or Chepstow and Raglan.

Quite often the history of these castles reads like a story taken from a gothic novel. There is suspense and mystery paired with the touch of the supernatural. The echo of receding footsteps in a long corridor or the eerie breathing sounds of a visitor from the world beyond will send a cold shiver down a person's spine.

The saying is that most of these castles are haunted. Anyway, who believes in ghosts in this time and age? There is no place for ghosts in an age of science and reason. So the visitors are completely safe in the ancient castles. Well, yes, but there is a lingering doubt somewhere in the soul. Maybe the castles are not so safe after all.

Abergele, Conwy
The beautiful lady in red of Gwrych Castle
Have you seen the scary ghost who rattles so furiously with a chain? Even if you have this is nothing compared to the skeleton in the hooded robe that sometimes manifests itself in

the doorway. It is rumoured that the skeleton also carries a scythe and that it knows how to make good use of it. Visitors to Gwrych Castle who hope to come across such terrifying characters in the building will be disappointed. The ghosts of this relatively modern castle in Abergele are pretty normal, people like you and me. That is of course also what they were when they were still alive. They are undeniably normal, but that does not mean that they are dull and insipid spooks. Their attraction lies in their normality, which at the same time throws up a multitude of ordinary questions.

Questions in turn have a habit of creating mystery, even if they are only questions concerning the identity or the death of a person. It is the mystery of day-to-day life that makes the ghosts of the castle attractive. In a manner of speaking each of the spectres has a story to tell. One begins to wonder who they really were.

Who, then, was the pretty lady in red with the strikingly blue eyes whose ghost often roams through the castle? Death did not manage to take away the lustre from her beautiful eyes, but it took away her history. It took away her name and her voice. It took away her laughter and also her tears. The lady with the beautiful eyes died an untimely death. It is rumoured that she lost her life accidentally in a fox hunt.

The blue-eyed lady does at least not lead a lonely existence. There is always the ghost of a lady in white with whom she can have a chat if she wishes to. It is known that the White Lady was interred in unconsecrated ground. This is quite likely the reason why she haunts Gwrych Castle. Some researchers have put forward a different theory: they believe that the White Lady has returned to the castle because she loved it so much during her lifetime.

Peter Southgate has strong childhood memories of the White Lady. As a young boy he used to spend the summers in one of the flats at the castle where his father worked as an organist. The lady in white showed herself to every member of the family. Her appearance never spread fear and terror. On the contrary, the Southgates felt that the ghost was friendly and likeable. While the Southgates had frequent encounters with the lady in white they apparently never noticed the ghost of the elegant gentleman who often appears together with a female spectre in the Emily Tower. The two spirits are believed to be husband and wife.

There is nothing that frightens us more than the unknown. It seems to be easy to get used to ghosts that physically appear from time to time. It is then obvious to the eye that no danger emanates from them. But what about entities that remain in the dark? Their presence can still be felt but they cannot be seen. There is always an unnerving aspect to invisibility.

Thomas Rice, who was the castle's caretaker in the 1930s, felt watched by a presence whenever he passed by the library in the evening. He often noticed that objects had been moved around in the library overnight when he checked it in the morning. This was technically impossible. The caretaker was in charge of the only key to the library. It was also obvious that no attempts were made to force the door open. Despite its creepy nature, the invisible watcher has been described as friendly.

In the 1980s a woman and her little dog had an encounter with the uncanny watcher when she stayed at Gwrych Castle. She was given the Telescope Bedroom on the second floor of the Round Tower. The invisible presence invaded her bedroom on a number of occasions. She never panicked for she knew in her heart that the ghostly visitor was well disposed towards her. Her little dog was of a different opinion: it took an instant dislike to the ghost. The dog seemed to be able to see the spectral entity and barked and snarled at it.

Another noteworthy incident occurred while the woman

was staying at the castle. One night a strange swishing sound disturbed her sleep. The corridor in front of the Telescope Room resounded with hundreds of short-lived swishing noises. Although she was understandably quite afraid she felt compelled to check out the corridor for her own safety's sake. When she entered the corridor dozens of bats were whirling around in it. The tower is not usually the home of a host of bats. Did their appearance coincide with the haunting of the invisible presence or did the ghost attract them?

Sometimes the ghosts of Gwrych Castle leave the building for a stroll. Elizabeth, who lives in Abergele, was quite surprised when she noticed three ghostly figures in front of the castle, a woman and two men. The spectres were dressed in medieval robes that had gone greyish white with age. Her witness statement is of particular interest. It is known that Gwrych Castle was built in the first quarter of the nineteenth century and belonged to Lord Hesketh and his wife Lady Emily Esther Ann. It is therefore of comparatively recent origin. How does that match the presence of medieval spooks? Do they come from a building that substantially predates the modern one? Have they, so to speak, just done a house-move?

When these three ghosts have a cosy day at home instead of wandering around in the neighbourhood of the castle they can be quite noisy. They open and close the windows of the building and the hallways reverberate with their footsteps.

Nathan Regan, who used to be a manager at Gwrych Castle, claimed to have frequently heard these inexplicable ghostly sounds. At times the whole castle resounded with phantasmal rattles and creaks. The noises were so loud that he could even hear them through the walls and floor of his flat at the castle.

Beaumaris *(Biwmaris)*, Anglesey
The spectral choir of Beaumaris Castle
Do you like music? Do you maybe even have a preference for classical music and Gregorian chant in particular? If that is indeed so, Beaumaris Castle will be a real treat.

It is said that the sound of ghostly chanting haunts the chapel area of the castle. The chanting has even been recorded on audio recording equipment. There is no apparent source to which the chanting can be attributed. When the chanting occurs there is no one present other than the witnesses.

The mysterious watcher-in-the-dark that haunts the sombre corridors of Beaumaris Castle has never been seen, but its presence can always be distinctively felt. The feeling of being watched is almost omnipresent. Unlike the benevolent invisible presence at Gwrych Castle, the watcher of Beaumaris is unpleasant. This uncanny spectral entity invades the emotions of the visitors and causes quite often a sensation of great loneliness in them.

Bodelwyddan, Denbighshire
A cup of tea with a ghost at Bodelwyddan Castle
If you have not got a skeleton in your wardrobe you may have one in your cupboard. If that is not enough it could also be the wall or rather behind the wall. Sure, that's a good place to hide your skeleton, much better than the wardrobe. It stands to reason that a wardrobe is not so effective when it comes to keeping out the odour of decomposition. You would need plenty of air-freshener. It is a safer option to hide the corpse behind a wall. Whoever hid the corpse that was discovered in the nineteenth century behind one of the walls at Bodelwyddan Castle must have thought along those lines. On the other hand, who can say what exactly happened all these many years ago?

The castle is old, and whatever occurred centuries ago

must by now be shrouded in mystery or completely forgotten. Bodelwyddan Castle was built around 1460. Even before the construction of the castle the site was inhabited. There is some evidence to suggest that there was a house on the site before Bodelwyddan Castle occupied it. Since then it has had various different rôles. In more recent decades it was used as a hospital during the First World War. In the 1980s the castle was transformed into a museum and art gallery with a historic house. Suffice it to say that the castle has picked up a ghost here and there.

Should we start with the Lilac Lady? Maybe not – it had better be the lady in blue, for not much is known about the Lilac Lady.

If you are lucky you can have a cup of tea with the Blue Lady. She just loves to appear in the Tea Room. This may present a bit of a problem if you are a coffee drinker. The scent of coffee will probably not attract her. She is also somewhat set in her ways, as the out-of-fashion mob cap she likes to wear proves.

If you have a love for the Victorian period you will have a real field day when you visit the castle. A number of Victorian ghosts have found a luxury home in the castle. They include a spectral lady who sometimes materialises in the Sculpture Gallery and a few child ghosts who can be seen all over the building.

Unlike the hound of the Baskerville Hall Hotel, who appears to be somewhat of a ruffian, the canine ghost of Bodelwyddan Castle has a philosophical streak. This spectral dog loves to appear in the castle's library. He must clearly be quite educated. What is more, he may well be even bigger than the hound of Baskerville Hall. After all we are dealing with an Irish wolfhound. Maybe the wolfhound is even a connoisseur who enjoys *la dolce vita*. Why else should the library often be filled with the scent of fine cigars? Imagine him sitting on a posh chair with a Cuban cigar between his teeth, musing over an old leather-bound tome. The saying is that he just loves French cognac, aged and mellow brandy. Unfortunately, some critics doubt the veracity of this theory. They believe that the scent of cigars is caused by the ghost of a man who has sometimes been seen in the library. Upon reflection one could ask whether there is a connection between man and dog.

Sometimes history relents and shows a bit of kindness. It does not always take away names and personality. For this reason we know the names of the two female ghosts, Elizabeth and Margaret, who have frequently been seen at the castle. Little, apart from her name, is known about Margaret. More is known about Elizabeth. This friendly female ghost was once a teacher.

As one century followed another the castle had many different rôles. During World War I it was used as a recuperation centre for wounded soldiers. Although the nurses did their very best to help the injured soldiers, not all of them survived. Thus the spirit of one of the deceased soldiers regularly returns to the castle. What is it that brings him back? Is it the shock and confusion of the violent nature of his death that compels him to haunt the building? Or is it maybe a last 'farewell and thank you' visit for the nursing staff?

During the course of a long life many misfortunes happen. It is known that an elderly woman died as result of an accident in the building. The untimely death and the shock of the accident have made her spirit restless. She can be seen wandering through the castle.

Cellars are the stuff the dreams of ghosts are made of. If you want to advance in the spectral hierarchy you must aspire to become a cellar ghost. And right enough the castle has two cellar ghosts, a man and a boy. We don't know about the boy, though. He may only be an apprentice ghost, not a fully-fledged one, so to speak.

Ghosts can create all sorts of phantasmal effects. What about a sudden drop in temperature? That is really good. Some ghosts would argue that this is heart-attacking spooking. And while we are at it you could just as well play some music. Most people like the sound of a harp but they may feel differently when it is a spectral harp.

If that does not work you must touch them. The sudden and unexpected touch of an ice-cold hand works wonders, as some witnesses can testify. Be it as it may, for some of the ghosts at Bodelwyddan Castle all this is stuff and nonsense. They prefer something a bit more solid and tangible. Strangulation! And indeed one of the spectral entities has been known to attack visitors. Whether the strangler is identical with the grey mist that sometimes appears in one of the rooms and makes people feel ill cannot be established without doubt.

All the spectral hullabaloo in the castle is too much for an unidentified lady in black and number of phantasmal children. They prefer a bit of privacy and have chosen to lead a life apart. You can be sure to meet them in the surrounding area of the castle.

Boverton *(Trebefered)*, Glamorgan
Lady Hadwisa of Boverton Castle

Some people do not seem to take the marriage vow of 'till death do us part' seriously. In their thinking it is rather 'till ambition or greed do us part'. Why else should John Lackland have got rid of his wife Hadwisa, a woman who apparently loved him dearly?

Well, yes, why? Was there not this little heiress from France, Isabella of Angoulême? And hey presto, that gave you a few gold coins in your pockets. But what about Hadwisa? Have you ever thought about her? How much you hurt her? The pain she felt and the tears she shed? Does that mean anything to you, John? The saying is that when things went wrong you came running to her and that she was kind enough to hide you. Now there is a woman! But what did you do to her? No wonder that the spirit of Hadwisa is upset. And indeed, Hadwisa has returned to haunt Boverton Castle.

The locals refer to her spirit lovingly as Wissie. The tragic course of her marriage is probably the reason why she remained earth-bound after her death. John Lackland divorced Hadwisa so that he could get married to Isabella of Angoulême. The unfortunate Hadwisa withdrew to Boverton castle and, to all appearances, continued to love her former husband with all her heart.

At the beginning of the nineteenth century workmen saw a tall regal lady in black with long dark hair while they were busy in the castle. When the workmen realised that her style of dress was from a bygone period they instantly knew that they had seen a ghost. The phantom woman seemed rather distraught and emitted sobs and sighs and wandered aimlessly about. She appeared many times to the workmen and communicated her pain and distress to them. The haunting is so strong that even after the workmen had completed their demolition work the ghost lingered around and was seen by a number of witnesses.

Bridgend *(Pen-y-bont ar Ogwr)*
The Blue Lady of Dunraven Castle
How can a haunting be explained? One of the theories is that the natural stonework of old buildings acts like a video recording device. It is thought that some magnetic field in the stones recorded events of the past and releases them under certain circumstances. Dunraven Castle is an argument against this theory. There are no stones left to show us a film recording of the past. Dunraven Castle was demolished decades ago. Even more to the point, the last Dunraven Castle was not a real castle but a building from the nineteenth

century topped by castellation. Yet, the site where the edifice once stood is still haunted. The phantasmal lady in blue who appears in the area of the former castle is reality. Since the demolition of the building she has been spotted several times.

Detailed descriptions of encounters with the lady in blue have survived the passage of time. It is most of all known that she brings with her a strong fragrance of mimosa whenever she shows herself.

During the First World War the castle was used as a convalescent home. In April 1917 a nurse arrived at the castle and was given the Amber Room. One night she awoke because she felt somebody softly touching her face. She thought that there was also a rustling sound. She immediately had a good look around and noticed a small elderly lady in a light blue dress standing near the door. The nurse was too frightened to leave her bed. She just stayed there watching the phantom. After a while the Blue Lady walked over to the fireplace. In the end the nurse mustered enough courage to turn on the light. As soon as the light came on the ghost disappeared. The Blue Lady left behind an all-permeating smell of mimosa.

The nurse had yet another brush with the Blue Lady. One night after reading a bit in a book she switched off the light and bedded herself down to sleep. Before she could even fall asleep the room was filled with the scent of mimosa. When the nurse looked towards the fireplace she could clearly make out the Blue Lady. The phantom lady sat peacefully on a chair beside the fireplace.

Sad to say that there are no nurses at the castle now, and as a consequence of this the Blue Lady has no human company these days. Neither is there any fireplace left to offer her some comfort: the fireplace she seemed to like so much disappeared when the castle was demolished. But there is always the spectral lady in green she can associate with when she gets too bored.

In *Haunted Castles*, Marc Alexander claims to know that the site where Duraven Castle once stood is also the haunt of a Green Lady. Despite extensive research which even took him to the British Museum where he studied books on castles he was unable to establish the identity of the Green Lady.

The exploits of Thomas Wyndham, if exploits they can be called, have little to do with the 'dead man's chest' in the old song, but there was most likely a drop of aqua vitae of some sort involved here and there, if not a 'bottle of rum'. Thomas would have needed something to keep him warm when he was out in a cold night to follow his trade as a beach pirate. Although the grim beach pirate died long ago he is still with us in a way. His ghost sometimes appears in the area of the former castle. Here then is the story of Thomas Wyndham.

Wyndham who was the master of Dunraven Castle amassed a fortune by plundering stranded ships. Eventually his love for gold became so strong that he was no longer satisfied with looting naturally stranded ships. He became a beach pirate and lured passing ships to their doom on stormy nights. But though he had gold in plenty, Wyndham was not free of worries. His wife had given birth to many children, but only one son survived. He loved his only child beyond measure. Only the best was good enough for his son. Wyndham had it in his mind to hoard an immense treasure for the child. In order to accomplish this he resorted to even more ship-wrecking. He tried to conceal his criminal activities from his son as best as he could, and for that reason the son was sent abroad for three years to complete his education.

In the meantime Wyndham planned to create a fortune for his son by looting more ships. Numerous ships followed the light of the lantern he waved on the beach, and were shattered on the rocks. Shortly before the return of his son Wyndham decided to give up ship-wrecking. Just one more time he went out to lure a ship into dangerous waters where it would inevitably run onto rocks. He had his wish that night, another ship stranded. In the morning he returned to inspect the wreck. There were no survivors.

Wyndham fainted with shock when he discovered that one of the dead was his son. The master of Dunraven was a broken man and died of insanity soon after the fateful event. He now haunts the beach and the spot where his castle once stood. On tempestuous nights his ghost sobs and wails in mental anguish.

Caergwrle, Flintshire
The elderly lady of Caergwrle Castle
The phantasmal elderly lady who haunts Caergwrle Castle seems to be really familiar with the little trick of walking through closed doors. One witness, a local woman, caught a particularly good glimpse of the ghostly lady and was therefore able to describe her in detail.

The woman was on her way home around 10 o'clock one evening. The journey to her house took the woman past the back of the castle, where she noticed an old and bolted door in the wall. Of a sudden somebody walked right through the door without opening it. It was the ghost of an elderly woman dressed in a black cloak. The phantom also wore a black hat which was rather similar to those worn in the Salvation Army. The spectral lady walked away but her feet did not to touch the ground. She seemed to glide through the air. After a while the ghost reached a small gate and disappeared.

Caernarfon
The phantom soldiers of Caernarfon Castle
It is rumoured that the whole region of Caernarfon is haunted because of its violent past. However, the most haunted place in the area is thought to be Caernarfon Castle.

In the truest sense of the word an army of ghosts haunts the castle. Sometimes the shades of soldiers who belonged to an old English garrison appear in the ancient building. These soldiers are ready for battle. They always manifest themselves fully armoured, with their weapons drawn.

A visit to the castle offers the prospect of dining with royalty. It also clearly demonstrates that Lord Death respects neither wealth nor rank. A few centuries ago Lord Death had a brief chat with a king who can now be seen wandering around in the castle as a ghost. The spectral king always wears a long cloak and carries a sceptre and a crown adorns his head.

By the way, if you happen to come across a quantity of bluish vapour or mist in the corridors of the building there is nothing to be worried about. It has nothing to do with worsening weather conditions either. The mist eventually turns into a spectral woman. The woman in blue also likes a good day out. She has often been observed strolling around in the courtyard.

Caerphilly *(Caerffili)*
Princess Alice of Caerphilly Castle
The nature of the legend of Caerphilly Castle is somewhat Shakespearean. It includes cabals, deception, disloyalty, betrayal and death. Such overpoweringly negative actions have a habit of creating a haunting. Caerphilly Castle is indeed a haunted place.

The spirit of an unfortunate woman in green has been spotted on many occasions in the building. It is said that this is the ghost of Princess Alice. Legend has it that while her husband, Lord Gilbert De Clare, was on a campaign abroad Alice became enamoured of Gruffudd the Fair, a Welsh prince, the Prince of Brithdir. He mentioned the love affair in a confession to a monk who betrayed him to his lover's husband. The enraged husband banished Alice to France and persecuted Gruffudd. The Welsh prince had time enough to take revenge on the treacherous monk before he fell into the hands of Gilbert De Clare. Gruffudd seized the monk and hung him from a tree. The site where the monk found his untimely end is now known as Monk's Vale. Eventually de Clare caught up with the prince and had him executed. To complete his revenge he sent a messenger to France to inform Alice of the execution. The news distressed her so much that she dropped dead on the spot. As a result of those tragic events Alice's spirit began to haunt the castle. Sometimes her ghost appears together with the ghost of a man in armour ...

One of the towers is haunted by the fragrance of perfume. The inexplicable presence of the phantom perfume frightens the security guards of the castle so much that they refuse to patrol the tower. It has been argued that this is the scent of Princess Alice's perfume.

Beautiful lady in red, who are you? While it is known that the lady in green was once Princess Alice nobody has ever been able to establish the identity of the Red Lady. One should think that this was not necessarily a complicated task, because the lady in red visits the castle with relative frequency and thus gives the researchers plenty of time to study her. Yet up to the present day she has managed to conceal her identity.

If you like a tasty mug of ale you will find excellent drinking companions in the ghosts of the ancient soldiers who can sometimes be seen walking back and forth on the battlements. A member of a local theatre group, Hazel, once had an unusual experience during an open-air performance of Hamlet. She is a skilled seamstress and the wife of the theatre's director. Hazel's task was to make, mend and prepare the costumes. She worked in a small room near the battlements. There was a strong oak door that allowed access to the battlements.

On a pleasant day in July Hazel was busily working on some costumes in the tiny room when of a sudden the oak door behind her began to shake violently in its frame. At the same time the temperature in the room dropped considerably. The incident frightened Hazel so much that she escaped from the room and ran downstairs to seek help from the actors. When they had heard what Hazel had to say the actors went to examine the oak door only to find it safely locked. They also found out that all other doors leading to the battlements were locked too. As all passages to the oak door were blocked, the only way to access it would have been by swimming the moat and scaling the giddy heights of the castle's wall. Are the ancient soldiers the cause of the haunting? It is known that they still patrol the battlements. Were they on a patrol when Jane saw the oak door shake in the frame? Should the door have been wide open, in the opinion of the soldiers? Did they try to force their way in when they found that the door was locked?

Caldicot
The hooded monks of Caldicot Castle
Caldicot Castle is definitely haunted by spectral sounds, but the source of these noises has so far remained hidden. Who is behind the haunting?

There may be a link between the phantom sounds and the mysterious lady in grey whose ghost sometimes wanders through the castle. However, it could be argued that a single person is not capable of generating so many different sounds, even if that person is a ghost. It is more likely that the sound-haunting is caused by the spectres of the hooded monks who have been spotted in the building on a number of occasions.

Does the presence of the devout monks offer some comfort to the shade of a young boy who visits the castle off and on? It is much to be hoped. His life has not always been easy. It is known that the boy was a poor vagabond.

It is the fear of the unknown that scares us most. It is relatively simple to cope with the presence of a lady in grey or a group of spectral monks because they can be clearly seen. The sudden appearance of a hazy dark shadow is a different matter. We do not know what dangers it holds, if any. Shadowy ghosts have been seen repeatedly in the Gatehouse Banqueting Hall. It is thought that the presence of the unknown has greatly contributed to the Hall's reputation as the most haunted part of the castle.

Whatever haunts Caldicot Castle has a particular effect on the security dogs. The dogs tend to shun the castle's keep. On full moon nights the dogs will not even walk over the drawbridge.

Cardiff
The Phantom Coach of Cardiff Castle
Who enters a house by way of the fireplace? Santa Claus! Correct! Alas, poor old Santa has lost his monopoly. He has a competitor.

The ghost of the second Marquis of Bute, who died in 1848, has returned from the grave. He is now active in his former home. The spectre of the Marquis often appears in the library, which he enters by way of the fireplace. He leaves the library by walking through a wall which is about two metres thick. The wall leads on to a hallway. Once in the hallway the ghost walks through another wall behind which lies a chapel. The final part of the tour leads the spectre to the room in which the Marquis died.

The ghost has been described as tall and wearing a red cloak. The red-cloaked phantom has also been seen near the top of the stairway.

The ghost in the main dining-hall of Cardiff Castle keeps to a regular timetable. At a quarter to four in the morning exactly, invisible powers open and close the doors of the dining hall and the lamps are turned on and off. Some people just love to start early in the day. The noisy visitor from the world beyond is thought to be identical with the ghostly personage Edward Rees once saw in the dining-hall.

Mr Rees, the custodian of the castle in 1975, had a brush with the phantom of the dining hall. Mr Rees was clearing up the dining hall when he became aware of a man in the doorway on the other side of the room. Mr Rees approached the stranger and politely asked if he could help him. The stranger turned around and disappeared. The haunting of the stranger has been verified by Mr Rees's children and one of their friends who stayed with them overnight. They saw a man looking at them in their bedroom who just vanished before their eyes. After the appearance of the ghost the room was troubled by poltergeist phenomena.

The storeroom near the dining hall is also haunted. The somewhat shapeless ghost of a woman in a dirty white skirt sometimes appears in the storeroom and moves around objects. Although the phantom woman is a bit hazy there is nothing dangerous or threatening about her.

This cannot be said of the ghost known as Sarah. Her appearance spreads fear. The frightening aspect about her is that she has no face.

The lady in white who haunts the attic area of the castle cannot be compared to Sarah. She is not faceless. Nevertheless her appearance is accompanied by unpleasant side-effects. A feeling of great sadness emanates from the White Lady and affects those who meet her.

In the 1960s the attic contained several studios where students of music could practise their art. Jane, a student of music at the Welsh College of Music and Drama, arrived at the castle on a May afternoon where she had rented a studio in the attic for an hour to practise on the piano. Jane had hardly begun when she heard the door behind her open and close. She turned round expecting to see one of the music or drama students. Instead she saw a young woman in an elegant, long white trailing dress. The lady in white walked over to the window and vanished. Jane looked for a natural explanation and hit upon one. She thought that the lady in white was a drama student who had slipped out on the roof to learn her lines in peace as the roof was open to the public. Yet, some doubt remained. Jane went after the mysterious young woman. She spotted the lady in white immediately, but as she approached her the lady vanished. Jane noticed that the manifestation of the White Lady was accompanied by a deep feeling of sadness.

Imagine you are peacefully walking through the night to get to your car. The traffic has died down and the silence of the night surrounds you. The stars are shining and you are somewhat lost in thoughts. Of a sudden you hear the clattering of hooves and as you look up you see a coach racing towards you. That must indeed be a scene from a horror film. Sometimes scenes from a horror film become reality, as the following eye-witness account proves.

Dylan was on his way home around half past four in the morning after a night out. He had not touched any alcohol as he was driving. In order to get to his car Dylan had to walk around the castle. When he had reached the Gate House he could hear horses and a jingling sound. He could also hear somebody shouting in an Irish accent. Of a sudden a majestic four-in-hand appeared some distance in front of him. The magnificent coach made straight for Dylan but did not hit him. It turned before any contact was made and disappeared through the castle gates.

It is rumoured that the tall gentleman who haunts the park of Cardiff Castle must have a good tailor. Regular shops would probably not be able to provide him with suitable clothes. Suffice it to say, the spectre is nine feet tall.

Cardiff

The grief-stricken Cavalier of Castell Coch

The ghosts of Castell Coch in Tongwynlais, near Cardiff, appear to be almost indestructible. They managed to survive the fire that ravaged the previous building and have come back to haunt the new castle. On the other hand it is tempting to argue that this was by no means an accomplishment – after all, they were already dead when the fire struck.

Even the spectre of a Cavalier who was first noticed in the nineteenth century is still there. At that time a lady and her two elderly servants occupied five rooms in the castle. One night the lady awoke to find a finely dressed Cavalier standing near her bed. The lady was not frightened, for she felt that the ghost meant no harm. The grief-stricken expression on the Cavalier's face evoked a feeling of great sympathy in the lady. She rose from her bed to console him. When she approached the Cavalier he turned and disappeared through a door in a dark corner. The lady followed him but when she tried the door she learnt that it was locked and bolted. She did not mind the company of the ghost. She rather liked him.

It is believed that the Cavalier owned the castle during the Civil War. The saying is that he had amassed and hidden an immense treasure in the secret underground vaults of the castle and that he then died in an accident. The barrel of a cannon exploded when he stood next to it. He did not survive the explosion. The violent end can be seen as a motive for the haunting. However, an alternative would be to suggest that the Cavalier had hoarded up the treasure to help his king. When he died the secret of the treasure was lost for ever. The thought of having failed his king could well have made his ghost restless.

The ghost of the grieving lady in white is less respected than the Cavalier. Her presence seems to cause a feeling of fear. The White Lady's name has been given as Dame Griffiths.

It is said that the cause of her grief was the accidental drowning of her young son in a lake in the vicinity of the castle. She never got over the loss of her son and died broken-hearted soon after the incident. Her frequent appearances frightened the widowed Lady Bute so much that she moved away from Castell Coch.

The White Lady is still very active. She was recently seen in September of the year 2007. A witness, Mark, spotted her near the woodland close to the castle. Mark noted that her clothes were quite old-fashioned and faded in colour. At that stage he did not realise that he had met a ghost. He thought that the woman in white was probably a member of one of the historical re-enactment groups that sometimes meet in the area. Of a sudden Mark noticed that the strange lady was floating in the air. Then, of course, it dawned on him that he had an encounter with a ghost.

Carew, Pembrokeshire
The tragic story of Princess Nest of Carew Castle
Much has been written about the age of chivalry. It has produced legends of heroic deeds and romantic tales. Those who were actually involved in these tales, like Princess Nest of Carew Castle, would probably argue that they were not really romantic but rather distressing and hurtful – that is, if they were still alive.

Henry I fell in love with Princess Nest who bore him a son. Eventually, Henry's love for Nest grew cold and he decided to rid himself of the princess. Henry arranged her return to Wales and a marriage to Gerald de Windsor. Carew Castle was part of her dowry. In 1109 Owain Cadwgan stormed the castle and took possession of it. Gerald of Windsor made good his escape, taking the children with him. For some unknown reason Nest stayed behind. De Windsor recaptured the castle six years later. By then Nest had two children by Owain

Cadwgan. De Windsor killed Owain in battle but died soon afterwards, probably from wounds received in the battle.

After her death Nest's ghost began to haunt the castle. Often the forlorn spectre can be seen wandering around as if searching for something or somebody.

It is rumoured that the shade of a deceased ape sometimes manifests in Carew Castle.

In the seventeenth century Carew Castle was the home of Sir Roland Rhys. He owned an unusual pet, an ape. One day the ape turned on Rhys and killed him. This tragic event led to a haunting. Both owner and pet now haunt the castle's north-west tower.

Perhaps the ghost of a former kitchen boy who troubles the kitchen area will have a chance to form a friendship with Sir Roland's pet ape at some stage in the future. Such a friendship would divert his attention from the kitchen. The staff would presumably receive the news with great joy for the spectral boy often plagues the kitchen with his pranks. Nothing seems to be safe. He throws around pots and pans.

The full moon hangs full and round in the sky and bathes the earth in its gentle light. The quavering 'ho … hoo … hoooo' of a tawny owl breaks the peace of the night. Another owl answers the cry from somewhere in the distance. Firm footsteps and the occasional clanking of metal echo in the moonlit darkness. A stranger is climbing a hill near the old castle. Brushwood and darkness conceal him well. The man reaches the top of the hill and the moonlight shines on him. Of a sudden the majestic figure is clearly visible. He is of a tall and powerful built. His hair is long and blond. The shining horned helmet on his head can barely tame his blond locks. His breast-plate glitters brightly and his long cloak billows in the breeze of the night-wind. His right hand rests on the pommel of a sword. The man is an ancient Celtic warrior. He is proud and strong.

The Celtic warrior of Carew Castle definitely exists. He has shown himself on various occasions.

Chirk *(Y Waun)*, Wrexham
The Green Lady of Chirk Castle

When the building manager of Chirk Castle moved into the flat where the castle's former nursery used to be he soon found out that the rooms were already occupied. He also realised that it is not so easy to dislodge these sub-tenants – they are ghosts. The manager and his family may not even like the idea of throwing out the spectres, for they are benevolent and make interesting company.

His daughter must have been quite perplexed when she woke up one night and saw a lady in green standing in front of her bed. The Green Lady keeps coming back. She has never been in any way threatening or intimidating and therefore comes across as rather friendly. It appears that the manager's daughter quite likes the visits of the amicable lady ghost. A good number of people would even envy her. She has what most of us only know from story time – a real live ghost story.

He refuses to grow up and is somewhat mischievous. This can only be the legendary Peter Pan. The phantasmal children who haunt the castle probably remind the manager and his family of Peter Pan from time to time. The child ghosts are harmless but sometimes they can be a bit impish. What a surprise the manager must have had when one of the ghosts pulled on his toes when he was asleep in his bed. But mostly the child ghosts do what all other children do. They play and run. Thus they can often be heard running down the corridor.

There is also the scraping and banging noise of invisible furniture being shoved around. The various members of the family have witnessed these noises at different times of the day. So far they have been unable to established whether this particular noise is also caused by the phantasmal children.

Coity *(Coety)*, Bridgend
The legend of Sybil of Coity Castle

A forlorn shade wanders through Coity Castle. The shade is the ghost of a beautiful woman. The phantom woman has been seen frequently on her tour through the castle. It is rumoured that the daughter of Morgan, Sybil, has returned from her grave to haunt her former home.

Morgan, a Welsh chieftain, fought a battle of survival against a Norman knight called Payne. The knight's dearest wish was to take over Morgan's castle. The Welsh chieftain made an attempt to solve the conflict without bloodshed. He offered Payne a peace settlement. If the knight married his daughter Sybil he would be given the castle without resistance. If he refused, the dispute was to be decided by single combat.

The Norman knight was an ambitious man. He readily agreed to the marriage and began to support the Welsh cause. Unfortunately, Payne was not faithful to his wife. He committed adultery on many occasions. Payne was cunning too. He replaced the original guards of the castle with his own men, which allowed him to leave the castle unobserved so that he could see his concubines. One night Sybil took revenge. She withdrew her husband's guardsmen and put her own soldiers on duty. Payne came back late that night but the guards refused him entry. When he declared that he was the very lord of the castle the soldiers went to fetch Sybil to identify him. Through the closed door of her bedchamber she calmly explained that she could not be moved to walk over to the gate because her husband was sleeping peacefully beside her. Why should he be out at that time of the night? Sybil declared that the man at the gate could therefore only be an impostor or an enemy. Payne was trapped. When the guards informed him of Sybil's reply he was left speechless. If he admitted that he was not in the room with his wife he would automatically put himself in a bad light. His secret would be revealed. The knight decided to spent the night outside in the rain.

Whether the legend of Sybil is true or not is not of great importance. What matters is the general idea of the story. Accordingly Sybil must have been unhappy. She was forced into an arranged marriage, practically bartered away like a piece of cattle. Sybil's husband never even thought for a moment about the results of being unfaithful to her. Her unhappy and difficult life easily provides a motive for a haunting.

Conwy
The faithful sentry of Conwy Castle
After all these years he is still there. Even after his death he continues to serve his master loyally and many people have seen him – the ghostly sentry of Conwy Castle.

The phantasmal guardsman of the castle seems to take his duty seriously. In summer and winter, in wind and rain, he walks to and fro on the battlements. He has only his cloak to keep him warm or shelter him from the rain. Do ghosts feel the cold?

On a December evening in the twenty-first century Bethan was on her way home. When Bethan passed the castle she felt watched of a sudden. She looked around but could not spot the uncanny watcher. As she walked on the feeling of being spied upon became stronger and stronger. Bethan was sure that there was something profoundly wrong. She looked over her shoulder again in the direction of the castle and saw the outlines of a large man in one of the towers. The contours of the stranger stood out clearly against the dim yellow background. He was clad in armour and wore a helmet. The source of the yellowish light appeared to be a candle.

Interestingly, Bethan did not notice a dark cloak on the

phantom. Thus the ghost Bethan saw differs considerably from the cloaked spectre. This may mean that Conwy Castle is home to yet another ghost.

Crickhowell *(Crughywel)*, Powys
The sorrowful White Lady of Tretower Castle

Sometimes a ghost can almost become like a friend for whose well-being one cares about greatly. A rather moving incident occurred when a woman was on a visit to Tretower Castle in Crickhowell, where she met a spectral lady in white.

The White Lady habitually shows herself in one of the castle's bedrooms where numerous visitors have seen her. One day she appeared to a female visitor who took an almost instant liking to her. She noticed that the phantom lady had beautiful green eyes and that they were full of sadness. A feeling of profound distress seemed to come from the White Lady. The female visitor left after seeing the rest of the castle but she could not forget the lady in white. The lady's sorrow had made a great impact on the visitor. Accordingly she returned several times to see how the White Lady was doing.

A lady in white has been seen strolling up and down the battlements. Unfortunately, it has not been possible to establish whether she is identical with the sorrowful green-eyed White Lady.

In the course of its long history Tretower Castle has had numerous different owners. The Vaughan family owned the castle for almost 400 years and it seems that when they finally sold it to the Parrys in 1783 not all of them left. At least one of the Vaughans stayed behind, a woman. She is somewhat elusive and does not show herself all too frequently. But off and on she can be seen walking around in the building. She is a bit intangible but that is nothing to be worried about. She is a ghost. The lady is said to be Sir Roger Vaughan's wife. Sir Roger was the first Vaughan ever to own the castle.

Lady Vaughan does not appear to have any interest in the

main bed-chamber. She leaves this room entirely to two other female ghosts. One of them does not stay in the chamber. Soon after appearing in the bedroom the unidentified ghost leaves and walks out into the gallery. Her spectral friend prefers to remain in the room. She just loves to sit near the window which goes well with her peaceful and tranquil nature.

If the ghosts in the main bed-chamber are so pleasant why should both visitors and staff feel so uncomfortable in this part of the building? It could be argued that this has nothing to do with this particular room. The feeling of discomfort may be caused by the haunting of the gallery which also affects the nearby stairway. There is something sinister and threatening about the ghost of the gallery. The entity that causes the feeling of threat and danger always remains invisible. The presence is so unpleasant that a few members of staff even refuse to go anywhere near the area. It is quite possible that this powerful ghost often extends its sphere of influence to the main bed-chamber.

Does the sinister presence of the gallery sometimes even take over the courtroom? It is hard to imagine that the atmosphere of doom that can often be felt in that room should be caused by the lonely ghost of a young boy who has been spotted there. The boy does not seem to be malevolent. He just sits peacefully near the door whenever he visits the courtroom.

Cydweli, Carmarthen
The phantom guardsman of Cydweli Castle
What would be the job description of a medieval guardsman of a castle? He would be described as a soldier stationed to guard against unauthorised entry or surprise attack. He would be employed to watch over the building. This is exactly what the sentry of Cydweli Castle does. When he has a look around or watches who enters the castle he is only doing his work dutifully. Nonetheless several visitors complained about being

watched by him. Not everybody seems to feel comfortable in the presence of a ghost. The guardsman of Cydweli Castle is undeniably a ghost. His preferred location is the gatehouse but that is typical of a watchman.

Often a man with a bow and a quiver full of arrows walks around in the castle. From the distance it would be easy to mistake him for a keen sportsman on his way to an archery session. Have another look. He also wears bits and pieces of armour. The archer is a guest from the world beyond.

The man in the hooded robe looks like an everyday average clergyman, a monk. He can often be seen roaming through the castle. The monk reveals his true identity when he suddenly vanishes. He is a ghost too.

Cydweli Castle also has several photogenic spectres. A phantom face appeared on a picture taken in the prison chamber. On another photograph the ghost of a small man can be seen standing in the castle.

Denbigh *(Dinbych)*
The White Lady of Denbigh castle
A lady in a white dress has been seen wandering through Denbigh castle on numerous occasions. She has also been spotted near the Goblin Tower. Sometimes she appears with a shimmering white light all around her body.

In a way the haunting of the lady in white is controversial. It has never been denied that there is a lady-haunting but the various witnesses cannot agree on the colour of her dress. A number of people saw her wearing a grey dress. Is the dress white or grey? The answer to this question is surprisingly easy. It is tempting to argue that there are two lady ghosts.

The castle is also home to a male ghost. As in the case of the lady ghost the details of the haunting have become slightly muddled up.

The son of Henry de Lacy, the builder of Denbigh Castle,

was alleged to have had a liaison with the daughter of a wealthy baron. There was no truth whatsoever in that rumour. Nonetheless, the young man was punished. For an offence he had not committed he was thrown off the Goblin Tower, a tower built to defend the castle's water supply. This grave injustice has made the man's soul restless. His ghost now haunts the tower that was instrumental in his death. The ghost has been described as dark and without form.

According to another local legend de Lacy's son was much younger when he died, just a mere child. The young boy fell to his death when the Goblin Tower was still under construction. He was playing on the scaffolding that surrounded the tower when he slipped and fell to his death. A number of visitors have seen a sad face looking out a window. It is thought that it is the deceased son's face.

Which version is correct? There may be a connection between the first account of the young man's death and the lady-haunting. It may be true that Henry de Lacy's son had a liaison with the daughter of a wealthy baron. His violent death would provide a motif for his lover to return as a ghost.

Ewloe, Flintshire
The mysterious singer of Ewloe Castle
Tramp! Tramp! Tramp! The trampling sound of marching feet. Boom! Boom! Boom! The dull sound of ancient Celtic war-drums. Hoo! Hoo! Hoo! The braying sound of horns. The sweet sound of harps mingles with the drums and the horns.

Surely this must be a description of a scene in a film. It is hard to imagine that such an incident could be reality but it is. Sometimes the sound of marching feet to the accompaniment of music manifests itself out of nowhere around Ewloe Castle. The nature of the music has been described as ancient Celtic. Are these sounds caused by deceased Celtic warriors who march to the tunes of their bards? If so the haunting would go back to the days of the ancient Celts, long before the construction of the castle.

Is the phantom singer who occasionally appears on the battlements part of the Celtic-warrior-haunting? The mysterious singer likes to be out in a rough night. When the wind blows and the rain falls in sheets and the thunder rolls his melodious voice rises above the din of the storm and fills the night with mystery and magic.

Has this sweet and mysterious singer returned from the grave to oppose the presence of evil? He must be aware of the glowing phantom dressed in white that wanders around on the battlements. It is said that a menacing aura of evil emanates from the phantom. Meeting this ghost may have fatal consequences. The ghost once so frightened a dog that the animal died of shock two days after the encounter. Is the singer the phantom's natural opponent? Does his sweet voice drive away the evil spirit?

The ghost of a nun who died in a bomb explosion during World War II is part of the haunting of Ewloe Castle. Sometimes she manifests herself in the surroundings of the castle. It is to be hoped that her prayers will have some influence on the evil phantom of the battlements.

Flint *(Fflint)*
The betrayer of Flint castle

Who is man's best friend? One might say that the answer is simple: it is the dog. If this were true King Richard II's dog would not have deserted him in an hour of need. As an alternative one might suggest that this is a case of 'blame it all on the hound'. Faithful Gelert and the Hound of Baskerville Hall are both victims of injustice and paid with their lives. And if they have not died they are still slavering and rightfully accusing their cruel murderers. Here then is the story of Math, the faithful hound of Richard II.

The ghost of Math, a hound often mentioned in history books, has returned from the grave to the site of his wrongdoing. Math, a greyhound, was known as the most loyal companion of King Richard II.

The historical background that led to the haunting is as follows. In 1399 the Earl of Cumberland persuaded the king to meet up with the Duke of Lancaster, Henry Bolingbroke, in London. On his way from Wales to London Richard was ambushed and taken to Flint Castle, where he eventually abdicated in favour of his rival Henry.

When Richard met up with Henry in the courtyard of the castle his faithful hound Math left him. Legend has it that Math would never look at anyone but his master. On that fateful day, however, Math had no time for Richard. The faithful hound deserted Richard and ran to greet Henry.

The betrayal of Richard appears to have made the hound's soul restless. Math's ghost often returns to the ruined castled and howls pitifully.

Haverfordwest *(Hwlffordd)*, Pembrokeshire
The vengeful rebel of Haverfordwest Castle

An eye for an eye and blood for blood does not appear to be a healthy philosophy, especially when the blood of an innocent victim is involved. The history of Haverfordwest Castle is particularly violent. At one point, in the truest sense of the above quote, the eyesight of a man was destroyed and a life taken in revenge.

During an uprising against the English occupation the governor of Haverfordwest Castle took a Welsh rebel captive. In order to learn the names of his companions the governor had him tortured. The saying is that the torture was so severe that the Welshman was blinded. However, even under such extreme torture the rebel stayed loyal to the Welsh cause and did not betray his companions. When he had recovered from his injuries he was allowed to move around freely within the confines of the castle. Why the rebel was given such liberty remains unknown to the present day.

After a while the Welshman became a close friend of the governor's young son. Unfortunately, deep down in his heart the rebel could never forget the harsh treatment he had received, and that was to have consequences. One day he snatched the boy and hastily made for the battlements. The governor begged the rebel to spare the young boy's life but the rebel knew no mercy. He threw the boy over the battlements and then jumped himself.

It is thought that the murder of the innocent child has caused the Welshman's ghost to be earth-bound. The ghost now haunts the ancient castle. Ghostly movements and shadows have been seen in the ruins of the castle.

Laugharne *(Lacharn)*, Pembrokeshire
The hound of Laugharne Castle
Rebecca Adams knew about the hound-haunting of Laugharne Castle but did not believe in it before she actually saw the dog.

One day when she was on her way to Laugharne a large dog approached her and sat down about 2 metres in front of her. The animal howled so eerily that Rebecca fainted. When she regained consciousness it was well past midnight and there was no trace of the dog. Rebecca was unharmed except for the shock.

Llanfihangel-y-Pennant, Gwynedd
The Loyal Sentry of Castell y Bere
He has often been seen standing in the evening twilight when the sky glows red in the light of the setting sun and the evening wind passes over grass and trees in a last cheerful blast. At this hour he steps out on the battlements and watches the

horizon and the departing sun. Tall and proud he stands on the battlements, immobile like a statue made of stone. The dark shadows of the night begin to shroud the sky and the man turns on his heels and melts away in the darkness. He is the loyal sentry of Castell y Bere, a ghost.

The lonely watchman seems to love the end of the day. At dusk he manifests himself on the battlements and remains there almost immobile until the sun has completely set and then he merges with the darkness of the night and disappears.

The exact cause of the haunting is not known but it has been theorised that the violent history of the castle has compelled the sentry's ghost to stay behind as a guard.

During its long life the castle has seen death and suffering. Llywelyn the Great is thought to be the founder of Castell y Bere. It is believed that the first stone was laid in 1221. A number of Welsh rulers conducted their campaigns against the advancing English forces from Castell y Bere. The castle thus occupies a central position in Welsh history.

After Edward I's triumph in Wales and the subsequent Treaty of Rhuddlan Llywelyn's brother Dafydd retreated to Castell y Bere, but the war was not yet over. In 1282 Dafydd rose in revolt and seized Hawarden. The uprising resulted in the death of Llywelyn near Builth. Dafydd carried on the fight from Castell y Bere, but he was eventually forced to flee to the mountains of Snowdonia where he was captured after some time. The war ended with the surrender of Castell y Bere to the king's forces. Edward I gave orders for the destruction of the castle in 1294.

It appears that the ghost of the sentry has survived the destruction of the castle. The guardsman has returned to protect the ruins of Castell y Bere near Llanfihangel-y-Pennant.

Llanrwst, Gwynedd
The hungry ghosts of Gwydir Castle

Hunger! Thirst! Darkness! Loneliness! But nothing is worse than the parching thirst. The unfortunate maidservant who was immured behind one of the walls in Gwydir Castle in Llanrwst must have thought those thoughts before she became weaker and weaker from thirst and starvation. Death finally came as a dear friend.

But she is not completely dead. Her ghost has stayed behind to point an accusing finger at her murderer, Sir John Wynn of Gwydir Castle.

Sir John was either the first or fifth baronet, the records are not excessively specific on this minor detail, had a liaison with a maidservant. When it became difficult to conceal the relationship Sir John murdered the maidservant and immured her in one of the walls. Legend has it that noxious fumes of the decaying body were noticeable in the surrounding area for months. The mouldering corpse did not stay in its dark prison.

Dressed in white or grey the ghost of the maidservant began to haunt the castle. A foul smell of decomposition emanates from the ghostly lady. Sometimes she announces her appearance with a sudden drop of temperature. The phantom has been known to touch those who cross her way. Oh you fortunate and lucky ones! One cannot get closer to a ghost than that. The spectral lady loves to manifest herself in a particular room which became known as the 'Ghost Room' for this very reason.

There is some archaeological evidence to support the account of the murder and the subsequent immuration. A large hollow space was found within the chimney breast near the Ghost Room. This is exactly the location where the body of the victim is said to have been buried. The smell of death is always strongest around this spot.

It is said that a murderer has a habit of returning to the scene of the crime. Even after so many years Sir John Wynn has not been able to shake off that habit. His ghost returns to Gwydir Castle on a regular basis. His spectre haunts the winding staircase that connects the Solar Hall and the Great Chamber.

History often repeats itself all over. Thirst! Hunger! Darkness! Loneliness! Those were most likely the last thoughts of the unfortunate maidservant before she died. The monk who got trapped in a subterranean passage that was linked with a secret room in the castle must have had similar feelings. Deprived of water and food the unlucky monk eventually died. Why does a monk get caught in an underground passage? The passage fits the description of what was once known as a priest's hole. In a hostile environment dominated by strict Protestantism a priest's hole was a secret hiding-place in which Roman Catholic priests could escape from persecution.

Hound of Baskerville Hall supporters will be pleased to hear that Gwydir Castle has its own hound haunting. There is no need to be jealous. Gwydir's hound will never surpass the glorious Baskerville Hound. Arthur Conan Doyle made sure of this by endowing the slavering little lap dog with eternal fame in his Sherlock Holmes story. The Baskerville Hound may not like to hear this but in a way the canine ghost of Gwydir Castle is superior to him. The existence of the Baskerville Hall ghost can be questioned because there is no tangible evidence to prove its veracity. On the other hand it is hard to disprove the occurrence of the hound haunting of Gwydir Castle as there is archaeological evidence to support the accounts of hound appearances in the castle. The bones of the dog spectre were found in the cellar of the building in 1995.

Dignified and at a regular pace and in a well ordered file

and side by side they strode through the night. Of all the possible spectral activities there is nothing that both frightens and fascinates us more than a phantasmal procession. In bygone days and often even nowadays the inhabitants of Galicia in northern Spain would lock their doors and shutter up the windows when the day of the arrival of the Phantasmal Procession was near. The castle has its very own phantasmal procession. Although it cannot compete with the Galician Phantasmal Procession it is still quite impressive. It usually appears near Sir John's arch on the Great Terrace. If you are lucky, if lucky it can be called, you can see it on one of your visits.

Llantwit Major *(Llanilltud Fawr)*, Vale of Glamorgan
The Dutch Sailor of Llantwit Major Castle
The ghost that troubles the castle of Llantwit Major is a Dutch sailor who lodged in the castle in the seventeenth century. The ghost of the Dutch sailor appears and disappears.

What is it like to die slowly, every day a little bit more? The body becomes weaker and weaker from starvation and the raging thirst slowly drives the mind insane. Weird visions begin to appear as the mind and the body gradually fate away. Finally you stumble and fall and there is blackness all around you. The lady in white who sometimes manifests in the castle died in exactly that fashion, murdered by her own husband. She died the slow and painful death of starvation, deprived of all food and water.

Manorbier *(Maenorb☐r)*, Pembrokeshire
The phantom ladies of Manorbier Castle
The old castle in Pembroke is known for its strong lady-ghost haunting. Both a lady in white and a lady in black appear in and around Manorbier Castle.

During the First World War a few soldiers were garrisoned

at the castle to keep watch on the coast. It was common practise to send the soldiers on guard two by two during the night. One evening a guard was taken off duty because of an illness. The remaining guard was promised a substitute. In the meantime he had to keep watch all on his own. The substitute soldier eventually arrived but greatly to his surprised there was no guard. It seemed that the remaining guard had disappeared. The perplexed soldier began to search for his lost companion. He finally found him unconscious on the village green. At first it was quite inexplicable why the guard should have strayed so far from the castle. In order to reach the village green one even had to jump over a stream.

When the soldier regained consciousness he reported that he had seen a lady dressed in white approaching him. In accordance with the rules he had challenged her, which she completely ignored. The White Lady kept coming towards him without saying a word. He was frightened and as a last resort he fired his rifle at her. The bullet could not harm her. It went straight through her body leaving her apparently uninjured. She then abruptly disappeared. The incident scared the guard so much that he ran towards the village for safety. He fell in the wild chase. The impact of the fall left him unconscious.

A lady in a black dress has been seen on a number of occasions near the castle. One of the witnesses, a lady who works for a nearby hotel, saw the Black Lady approaching the gate of the castle. The ghostly woman never reached the gate. She suddenly vanished.

The lady in black is tall of stature. She suddenly manifests in the middle of a path leading up to the castle's gate. She then starts to walk up to the gate and disappears before she reaches it.

Merthyr Mawr, Bridgend
The phantasmal wolf of Candleston Castle
One of the ghosts that haunts Candlestone Castle is thought to be lupine rather than canine.

In the area near the dilapidated castle in Merthyr Mawr some scenes of *Lawrence of Arabia* were filmed. One night technicians and security staff were working late in their camp near the wood beside the castle when they heard the howling of a dog. The dog appeared to be only a short distance away. Everybody naturally thought that the howling came from the guard dog. How mistaken they were. Some time later the security guard emerged from his caravan without his dog. The puzzled guard explained that his dog was too frightened to leave the caravan and that it surely had not howled. When they explored the area they saw a shadowy figure between the trees which they took for a big dog. Could it have been a phantasmal wolf? After all the name of the founders of Candlestone Castle, the Cantalupes, translates as 'Running Wolves'.

A ghost is not always bound to a specific building or location. Some ghosts move around considerably. A White Lady has made her home in the castle and the surrounding grounds. It has been suggested that the White Lady travels around in the region. Some researchers therefore believe that the same lady in white also appears in Ogmore Castle and Ewenny Priory.

Near the castle there was once a Celtic chapel whose grounds are still haunted. The site is littered with ancient sacred stones and stone crosses. A legend grew around a particular stone which was heavily decorated with carvings, the goblin stone. This stone was home to a ghost whose identity got lost or else was never known. It would appear logical to argue that there was a grave underneath the stone and that it was the grave that was haunted rather than the stone itself. The ghost would dash out of the grave and seize every passer-by. The phantom would then force those unfortunate people to embrace the stone on the tomb. As soon as the ghost's victims touched the stone their hands and feet stuck to it. They could regain their freedom by praying. Legend has it that the ghost is still around.

Merthyr Tudful
William Crawshay II haunts Cyfarthfa Castle
It is said that some members of the Crawshay family are linked with supernatural occurrences in the region. Thus Richard Crawshay, as seen in the article on the Rhymney House Hotel, appears to have been involved in an incident that has caused a haunting. His relative William Crawshay II is an active ghost who haunts Cyfarthfa Castle.

The castle was built in Merthyr Tydful in the early part of the nineteenth century. It was the residence of the Crawshay family, who were wealthy owners of ironworks.

William Crawshay II's grave can still be seen in Pontsticill. He seems to have had an unfavourable reputation for it is rumoured that he was put in the tomb upside down to stop his wicked soul from returning to this world. This method does not seem to have been very effective as Crawshay's ghost can be encountered all over his former home. Many witnesses felt strangely affected by the atmosphere around Crawshay's grave. It has been described as eerie.

Crawshay's ghost appears quite regularly in many parts of the castle. Now and then an invisible force moves around objects in his former bedroom. The supernatural occurrences in the bedroom have been attributed to William's spectre. It appears that he is also active in the Library. The doors of the Library inexplicably lock even when nobody is inside. It is believed that the ghost also creates all the other supernatural phenomena in the castle, inexplicable footsteps, slamming windows, cold spots and heaters that heat up on their accord.

Crawshay's ghost is not the only phantom in the building. The shade of a former servant, Mary O'Connell, has come back from the world beyond. Mary's sister Emily was also in the employ of the Crawshays. One day Mary died of pneumonia. It is said that Mary's ghost followed the grieving sister around in the building attempting to comfort her.

Miskin *(Meisgyn)*, Rhondda Cynon Taf
The Grey Lady of Hensol Castle

It is said that almost all castles in the world have at least one ghost. Hensol Castle in Miskin is definitely not the exception to the rule. On the other hand it would be correct to argue that the haunting of the castle is exceptional. While most spectres limit their activities to wandering around or wailing and sobbing, the ghost of Hensol Castle has a more direct approach. The phantom likes to touch people.

The 350-year-old castle has been transformed into a conference centre. Hensol offers a wide range of services which also include training courses for teachers. In 2002 Alice went on a one week training course for teachers of Welsh.

During the training week Alice had a brush with a ghost. One day when she went to the toilet she sensed that she was being followed. She naturally believed that the person behind her was another student. Alice opened the door and entered the room. At this point she looked over her shoulder and was surprised to learn that there was nobody at all behind her. Alice began to feel uncomfortable but nonetheless she went into one of the cubicles and locked it. Of a sudden Alice felt somebody touching her back. After this incident she rapidly left the toilet.

Alice thought it best to report the strange phenomenon to the reception desk. She was told that Hensol was haunted and that both staff and clients had witnessed the haunting. Alice also learnt that a Grey Lady has been seen in the building.

Newport *(Casnewydd-ar-Wysg)*
The giant ghost of Newport Castle
The ghost of Robert FitzHamon, who haunts Newport Castle in Gwent, is said to be unusually tall. It is therefore tempting to make light of the haunting, as most ghosts are of normal height. The giant spectre of Newport Castle must surely be a figment of one's imagination. In reality the situation is far more complicated. While giant ghosts are not the norm they still occur with relative frequency. In the story of the haunting of Cardiff Castle a giant ghost that sometimes appears in the park was mentioned. Across the border in England the huge ghost of Sir Goddard haunts Brede Place, north of Hastings. It can thus be argued safely that the ghost of Newport Castle is neither ridiculous nor incredible. It is a true haunting that has parallels elsewhere in the world.

But the haunting of the castle is unusual in more than one respect. The castle was built in 1172 by Robert FitzHamon, whose ghost is now active in the building. Since the first stone was laid the castle has changed its shape numerous times. During its long life the fortification was attacked on several occasions. As a consequence of this the castle is now in an advanced state of decay. Practically nothing remains of the original building substance. This stands in strong contrast to the theory that ghosts are but mere recordings in the stonework, comparable to a videotape recording. The original castle has disappeared but that does not stop the shade of Robert FitzHamon from appearing in the ruins.

Newport *(Trefdraeth)*, Pembrokeshire
The Lavender Lady of Newport Castle
Night. A time of rest. The man was in a deep slumber. Of a sudden a slight unaccustomed noise woke him. When the man opened his eyes he froze with shock. A woman he had never seen in his life stood before him. She was completely dressed in white. The man instinctively felt that the lady in white was

not from this world. He was too frightened to move or say anything. His eyes were fixed on the phantom. He expected the worst but the lady remained passive and peaceful. After a while she turned around and disappeared. He realised that the room was filled with the fragrance of lavender.

Something similar happened to Richard Hunter who lives at the castle. He woke up one night in his bedroom and saw a lady in white standing in front of him.

The White Lady is also known as the Lavender Lady. The scent of lavender can often be smelled in the building although there is never any lavender around. The occupants of the castle attribute this occurrence to the White Lady.

The lady in the white dress also appears on the banks near the castle. She can be seen walking over a low hill which leads on to Castle Street. The ghost's route is identical with the old castle path. In her lifetime the White Lady probably often walked down that path to the castle.

Ogmore-by-Sea *(Aberogwr)*, Vale of Glamorgan
The White Lady of Ogmore Castle

A man once chanced upon a lady in a white dress at Ogmore Castle who declared herself willing to share a treasure with him. She led him to the hiding place of a cache of gold, and it was agreed that each of them should take an equal share of the treasure. The man went away with his portion of the treasure while the White Lady's gold was left in the hiding place. Unfortunately the man was of a greedy disposition. He thought that he could just as well have the White Lady's gold. One night the treasure hunter returned to the castle and took the rest of the gold. He had almost made good his escape when the White Lady manifested herself. She fiercely defended her treasure. The word is that she had claws instead of hands. This may well have been an exaggeration. Narrated accounts of a particular event have a habit of becoming embellished as they are passed down from generation to generation. The claws of the woman in white may simply have been long fingernails when the legend of the White Lady of Ogmore Castle was first told. There is indeed some substance to this theory because there is an alternative account of the event in which the White Lady has no claws and does not even attack the thief. According to this account the gold robber simply felt a drop in temperature and soon after this the White Lady appeared. Instead of attempting to fight off the robber she simply chided and cursed him, then disappeared. The Lady's curse led to the untimely death of the villain a few weeks later. Be it as it may, in the ensuing brawl of the first account the White Lady severely injured the man. He managed to return home, but died a couple of days later of his injuries.

The haunting is still active. Even recently a lady in white has been seen frequently in the area. A few years ago a motorist nearly collided with her when he was driving on the B4524.

The White Lady may well be the ghost of the daughter of Maurice de Londres, who was the son of the first Lord of Ogmore. Lord Maurice once caught a Welsh nobleman poaching near the castle and brought him back to Ogmore to be tortured in front of the castle's inhabitants. The Welsh prince's valour and noble bearing greatly impressed the audience. It is therefore not surprising to learn that Lord Maurice's daughter rushed to the defence of the Welsh nobleman. It was her birthday and so she consequently begged her father to spare the prince's life as a birthday present. She also urged her father to give the prince a small hunting district. This wish was granted but there was a condition attached to it. Lord Maurice gave his daughter from sunrise to sunset to walk around a portion of land. The prince was to be given exactly that portion of land. Lord Maurice's daughter was not allowed to wear shoes on her walk.

This legend reveals a number of points that may well explain the haunting of Ogmore Castle. Ghosts often act as guardians: the White Lady of Ogmore Castle is the guardian of a treasure; Lord Maurice's daughter was a guardian to the Welsh nobleman. Ghosts often return to a place to which they were greatly attached when they were alive: Lord Maurice's daughter must have felt strongly attached to the piece of land around which she walked. She must equally have had a strong bond with the castle where she committed the heroic and memorable deed of saving the Welsh nobleman. It follows that Lord Maurice's daughter would have had more than one reason to return from the realm of the dead.

Pen-how *(Pen-h□)*, Newport
The Spectral String Quartet of Penhow Castle
The gentle sound of stringed instruments has always had the power to enchant an audience. Of late it seems that stringed instruments can also have an adverse effect on the listeners. One evening at Penhow Castle they were the cause of fear and amazement.

One night a number of people attended a dinner party at the castle and sat peacefully together when of a sudden a phantasmal string quartet appeared and began to play beautiful music. The ghosts soon vanished into thin air. While the dinner guests enjoyed the music they were still somewhat frightened and perplexed.

Sir Roger de St Maur, known as Seymour, is presumably the most famous past owner of Penhow Castle. Although Sir Roger passed away long ago he is still around. His ghost can often be seen wandering to and fro in the courtyard.

A former kitchen-maid sometimes returns to the castle. She haunts the Great Hall. Mr and Mrs Sherwood of Richmond had an encounter with her when they visited the castle in 1977. The Sherwoods noticed that the girl was in her teens and of short stature. The ghostly girl wore a blue-grey apron and kitchen clothes.

The Banqueting Hall is thought to be the most haunted part of the castle. The room oozes an atmosphere of tragedy which is believed to stem from a long-forgotten incident. Few details are known. The incident may not actually have occurred in the Banqueting Hall itself but in the bedroom above it. It has been established beyond doubt that a young girl was involved in some tragic occurrence that took place in the bedroom. The haunting may have spread from the bedroom to the hall underneath it.

It is not known whether the male phantom that sometimes appears in the Banqueting Hall played any rôle in the tragedy. The man may haunt the room for an entirely different reason. The shade is around forty years old and bearded.

Scenes with creaking stairs without anybody visibly walking on them are often used in horror and mystery films. At Penhow Castle such scenes have become reality and belong to everyday life. Invisible phantom feet make the castle's wooden staircase creak heavily. The phantom does not always remain hidden, and it is therefore known that the haunting is caused by the spectre of a woman.

The ghostly coming and going in the castle creates all sorts of supernatural sound and light phenomena like light orbs, the heavy tread of feet and knocking and rapping sounds as well as cold spots.

Penycae, Powys
The Opera Singer of Craig-y-Nos Castle
Craig-y-Nos Castle is of recent date and cannot even be considered a true castle. The original building was a Victorian country house which was given the appearance of a castle by the addition of a tower towards the end of the nineteenth

century. In those days the building was still called Bryn Melin. Craig-y-Nos Castle is home to a famous ghost.

The renowned opera singer Adelina Patti bought the former country house near Pen-y-Cae at the beginning of the twentieth century. She changed the building's name from Bryn Melin to Craig-y-Nos. Adelina spent many happy years in her new home. After her death Adelina's ghost began to appear in the castle she loved so much. Far from being a lonesome spook Adelina has illustrious and beloved company, the ghost of the Marquis of Caux, who was her first husband.

In 1919 the building was sold once again. It then served as a TB hospital for many decades. A number of patients who died of tuberculosis when they were treated at the castle have come back from the world beyond to haunt the edifice.

Port Talbot, Neath
The curse of Margam Castle
Ten little bottles are hanging on the wall and if one of them should accidentally fall there will be nine little bottles hanging on the wall. Who cares, that is just one bottle less. But what about the pillars of Margam Abbey? What if one of them should accidentally fall. That is a different matter altogether. It spells out disaster. Or at least so legend has it.

Margam Castle was once the proud family home of the Mansel family. Nowadays the name of this family is but a faint memory, a few lines in a history book. The name of the family has passed into oblivion and no direct member of this family is still alive.

It is said that the extinction of the Mansel family was due to a curse. In bygone days the Cistercian monks of Margam Abbey protected their abbey with a curse. If the pillars of the abbey's gatehouse were to fall, then the bloodline of the one guilty of this neglect would become extinct. The Mansel family apparently paid little heed to the curse and allowed the pillars to fall over. A few years after the fall of the pillars the last member of the Mansel family died. It appears that the monks who cursed the abbey are still around. Now and then several spectral monks manifest themselves in Margam Castle, probably in order to remind the present owner of the curse.

The phantom monks are not the only ghosts that haunt the castle. A White Lady often appears near the stone staircase. The saying is that a member of the Talbot family (who owned the castle after the Mansel family became extinct) fell down the stairs when she tripped over the hem of her skirt and died as a result of the fall. There is also an alternative version of her death in circulation. In this version she was pushed down the grand staircase and died. Sometimes the ghost of a man appears near the stairs. Is there a connection between the White Lady and the phantom man? Was he the one who pushed the lady in white down the stairs?

Another occupant of Margam Castle also died under dubious circumstances. A maidservant had an illicit relationship and became pregnant which was considered a disgrace in those days. Mothers who gave birth to children outside wedlock were shunned by society. Rather than face such a fate she committed suicide. According to another account the maidservant simply died in childbirth.

The ghost of a former gamekeeper, Robert Scott, has been seen by a number of witnesses. He was killed in a confrontation with a poacher. This unnatural death brought about by a cowardly deed has filled Scott with anger. His spirit is unhappy and therefore not yet ready to pass on. Often his anger is quite apparent. In fits of aggression Scott slams the doors of the castle with great force.

Not all the spectral occupants of Margam Castle are as ferocious as the gamekeeper. The phantom of a burly blacksmith that sometimes appears in the garden has a far milder temper. The smith is of a huge and impressive stature.

He is a harmless ghost who seems to enjoy the occasional stroll in the garden.

A merry bunch of spectral children haunt the corridors of the castle. There they can be seen flitting around as if they were still alive. Their style of dress reveals that the children must have lived and died in the nineteenth century.

Presteigne *(Llanandras)*, Powys
The bleeding ghost of Stapleton Castle

The legend of Stapleton Castle in Presteigne has all the components of a Shakespearean plot. It is a violent story that starts with an accidental death during a hunting trip followed by abduction, a sinking ship, stranded in a foreign country, loss of heritage, murder, the return of the avenger and finally also a ghost.

The master of Stapleton Castle died in an accident during a stag-hunt. He left behind his young wife and his son Everard.

The tragic events of Stapleton Castle really began when Lady Stapleton appointed a steward, Morgan Reese, to look after the castle. The greedy steward coveted the castle for himself. He devised a plan to rid himself of the young heir. Reese managed to persuade Lady Stapleton to send Everard to a boarding school. After a few months at the boarding school Everard received a letter in which he was told that his mother wished to leave the country to escape from the Civil War. He was to meet up with his mother in Cardiff. Everard walked straight into a trap. Once in Cardiff Morgan Reese's henchmen seized Everard and threw him on a ship which left the country with the young man on board. In the end the steward's evil plan failed because the ship sank in a storm. Everard was rescued by a vessel bound for North America. He eventually ended up in Virginia where he made friends with a widowed man and his daughter Mercy. After some time Everard got married to Mercy.

In the meantime Reese took full control of the castle. He slit Lady Stapleton's throat and spread the rumour that she had committed suicide.

After ten years of exile in America Everard and his wife returned to Europe. He joined the forces of Charles II and was knighted for his service.

Everard and Mercy finally reached Stapleton Castle. The castle had changed considerably in his absence. The young man felt like a stranger in his own home but most of all he was unable to locate his mother. Of a sudden Everard heard a scream that seemed to come from his mother's bedroom. The young couple hurried to the bedroom and were confronted by Lady Stapleton's ghost. The spectre had a horrid appearance. It was lying on the floor bleeding from the wounds Lady Stapleton had received in the final moments of her life.

Everard drew the right conclusion from the encounter with his mother's ghost. He challenged Reese but the brutal steward got the better of him. The young man was a prisoner once more. Just at that moment an old faithful servant, Pritchard, came in and grasped the situation in a split-second. He shot Morgan Reese without any hestation.

Charles II confirmed Everard's rights to the castle. The young man also revealed the truth about Lady Stapleton's death and the stain of suicide no more tainted her name. Nonetheless Lady Stapleton's ghost still haunts the castle. Perhaps she enjoys spooking. We all have our little shortcomings.

Raglan *(Rhaglan)*, Monmouthshire
The Librarian of Raglan Castle
It is thought that the librarian of Raglan Castle hid a number of valuable books during the Civil War to save them from destruction. Legend has it that the librarian concealed the books in an underground passage beneath the castle. He acted prudently; the Parliamentarians took Raglan Castle and left

the library in ruins. Even after his death the brave librarian continues to protect the books. His ghost returned as a guardian spirit and was even seen recently by a schoolgirl.

The courageous librarian may sometimes come across the ghost of a bard. The musician has been seen in the castle on a number of occasions, always wearing his professional attire. The presence of the bard may well have a link with Sir William Herbert who inherited the castle from his father in 1445. Sir William was a patron of the bards and welcomed them to his castle. It is quite possible that the spectre of one of the bards who used to visit Raglan has remained earth-bound and now haunts the castle. The saying is that the phantom bard loves to manifest himself in the library.

Rhuddlan, Denbighshire
The beast of Rhuddlan Castle

And they lived happily ever after. In the 'Beauty and the Beast' the heroine marries the beast who miraculously metamorphoses into a prince. The marriage seems to be a success. It is said that there are no divorce proceedings as yet.

But marrying a beast does not always pay off. Sometimes the rôles are reversed: there may be a beast hidden under the mask of a prince. Here, then, is what the legend of Erilda has to say.

Erilda of Rhuddlan Castle, a princess of north Wales, was to marry the prince of South Wales, a union which would have brought peace and stability to the two kingdoms. The wedding never happened because Erilda fell in love with a mysterious knight in black armour who had once rescued her when she got lost in a forest. The knight's manners were pleasant enough but little apart from his name, Werthold, was known about him. Eventually Werthold eloped with the princess. The escape was discovered and the garrison of the castle, Erilda's father included, pursued the lovers. The soldiers soon caught up with the couple. In the ensuing fight Erilda killed her own father by accident. Erilda was in shock and mad with grief. At this point Werthold shape-shifted and took on his true appearance. He turned into a scaly monster with a trident. The true Werthold was far from chivalrous; he was a malevolent being. He explained to the princess that it had all along been his intention to spoil the union between the two kingdoms by ruining the marriage. After that confession the knight murdered Erilda.

It is said that as a result of the tragic events at Rhuddlan Castle Erilda's ghost began to haunt the building.

The legend of Erilda cannot be completely true. Reality and mythology seem to have become mixed up. Yet, there appears to be more than a modicum of truth in the Erilda myth. The castle is haunted just as the legend claims. It is rumoured that the spectre of a woman wanders around in the edifice.

Roch *(Y Garn)*, Pembrokeshire
The belle of Roch Castle
With her dark hair and blue eyes Lucy Walters was indeed a belle. Her life story is not another version of 'The Beauty and the Beast'. It could rather be called 'The Beauty and the Greed' for it was an apparently ambitious and greedy man who brought about her downfall. Although Lucy passed away long ago she is still around in a manner of speaking. Her ghost haunts Roch Castle. The castle has always been Lucy's home. She was born at Roch Castle in 1630. Lucy's ghost is elegantly dressed in white. The white contrasts strikingly with her dark hair and blue eyes.

Lucy and Charles met when the future king was in exile on mainland Europe. They became lovers and she soon gave birth to a son – the future Duke of Monmouth. Three years later a daughter was born to the couple.

The relationship did not last for life – the lovers separated. Some time after the separation Lucy died, being only twenty-eight years of age. Two years later Charles returned to the throne his father had lost.

Lucy always claimed that she was legally married to Charles. While the couple may have been married Charles would have been forced to deny any such claim for political reasons. Charles was almost penniless. Money was what he needed most if he wanted to restore the monarchy. He was therefore forced to ally himself with wealthy families. Lucy was not affluent, which would have compelled Charles to distance himself from her. Yet the idea of a secret marriage to Lucy has survived and is supported by scores of historians.

What speaks for Charles is that he always acknowledged his son and treated him well. The future Duke of Monmouth was taken by force from Lucy and given a good education in Paris. Lucy stayed close to her son and lived in Paris where she died so young. It is no longer known where she was buried. Throughout her life Lucy claimed to be the legal wife of Charles. She professed she had the appropriate documents to support her claim. It is known that a number of those documents were destroyed by her enemies. In sum, all the ingredients for a haunting have come together. Lucy was quite likely a disowned wife and had her child taken away. Lucy must have been devastated when the documents that proved the legality of her claim were destroyed by her opponents.

The exact causes of Lucy's early death are unknown. It is justifiable to argue that she did not die from a sexually transmitted disease as was suggested at the time. She was a thorn in the side of the high and mighty. Her adversaries made every effort to besmirch her reputation.

Lucy has returned to Roch Castle to haunt the home of her childhood. She can be seen as a beautiful White Lady. The sound of running feet has also been heard. This sound may be connected with Lucy.

Ruthin *(Rhuthun)*, Denbighshire
The Phantom Knight of Ruthin Castle

Ruthin Castle, now a hotel, is haunted by a knight who lost a gauntlet. It is possible that the loss of the gauntlet had tragic consequences. It upset the knight so profoundly that he returned after his death to haunt the castle. Off and on a phantom knight in gleaming armour appears in the building. He is fully armoured but wears only one gauntlet. It is of particular interest to note that a single gauntlet was found in an excavation. Did the lack of the gauntlet lead to a serious injury which caused the knight's death? This could be a possible explanation for the haunting.

Ruthin Castle is also home to a lady in grey. There are two differing accounts of her fate. According to one version the haunting began in the fifteenth century. The Grey Lady was the wife of a steward. She found out that he was unfaithful to her. In a fit of rage she killed and decapitated him. The Grey Lady was found guilty of the crime and sentenced to death by beheading.

In another version things began in the reign of Edward I. The Grey Lady was married to an officer stationed at the castle. Her husband had an affair with a younger woman. It is known that the husband's paramour was a peasant. The spurned wife killed her rival. She was sentenced to death for the crime and buried in unconsecrated soil near the castle. She haunts the hotel's dining hall, which used to be the chapel of Ruthin Castle. Some witnesses have also seen her walking on the battlements.

St Athan *(Sain Tathan)*, Vale of Glamorgan
The White Lady of West Orchard Castle

West Orchard Castle in St Athan was the scene of an unimaginable tragedy. Centuries ago a young woman was tortured to death in a field near the castle. The agonising death of the young lady led to a haunting but it is not, as one should expect, the victim or one of the villains that has come back from the grave.

West Orchard Castle (also known as West Norchete Castle) was once the home of Sir Jasper de Berkerolles. Sir Jasper was married to Lady de Clare. Shortly after his return from a crusade Sir Jasper began to accuse his wife of adultery. He even claimed to have found out the identity of her alleged lover, Sir Gilbert d'Umphreville of East Norchete Castle. Lady de Clare denied the accusation because she was truly innocent. Nonetheless Sir Jasper meted out punishment. Lady de Clare was locked up in her room and left to starve to death. The servants disobeyed the order and smuggled in food.

When the cruel Sir Jasper realised that his plan had failed he had his unfortunate wife buried up to the neck in a nearby field where she was left to die of starvation and thirst. No one was allowed near Lady de Clare.

Legend has it that family and friends intervened in vain on Lady de Clare's behalf. Eventually Lady de Clare's sister was given permission to visit her every morning on the condition that she brought neither food nor drink to her sister. Lady de Clare's sister bypassed that order. Every morning on her way to the field where Lady de Clare was buried she always made sure that the hem of her long dress would soak up plenty of dew. Lady de Clare would then suck the liquid from the dress. However, the kindly act of her sister only prolonged the suffering of Lady de Clare. After ten days she died of hunger, cold and exhaustion.

It was too late when Sir Jasper learnt the truth: Gilbert d'Umphreville had indeed tried to persuade Lady de Clare into running away with him, but she had remained loyal to Sir Jasper and sent the unwelcome suitor away.

D'Umphreville soon took vengeance. He began to spread vicious rumours about Lady de Clare. Sir Jasper readily believed in the slanderous tales and condemned his innocent wife to death.

All facts considered one would expect to see Lady de Clare's ghost in the area. D'Umphreville and Sir Jasper, evil as they were, would also be good candidates for a haunting. However, neither of them has ever returned from the grave to haunt the castle. Yet there is a ghost: the ghost of Lady de Clare's kind sister. The suffering of her sibling seems to have distressed her so much that after her death her ghost began to appear in and around the castle. The ghost prefers to appear in the summer months and always at dawn – the time of the day when she visited her sister.

St Donat's *(Sain Dunwyd)*, Vale of Glamorgan
Lady Stradling of St Donat's Castle
Murder or grief? Is it a case for Arthur Conan Doyle? May be a bereavement counsellor would be a much better solution? It is not quite clear what circumstances led to the haunting of St Donat's Castle. Some researchers have come to believe that it was foul murder; others are quite sure that it was grief.

Be it as it may, the ghost of Lady Stradling has been seen in the castle numerous times. She is an imposing elderly lady who wears high-heeled shoes and a trailing long dress. It is rumoured that Lady Stradling was murdered at the Castle. The ghost often appears in the Long Gallery. She belongs to a category of ghosts known in the trade as 'crisis manifestation'. The appearance of the ghost always heralds the coming of a disastrous event.

As an alternative some researchers have suggested that the female ghost may be the grieving widow of Thomas Stradling who is thought to have died in a duel. In 1738, when he was twenty-eight years old, he decided to travel the continent together with his friend John Tyrwhitt. Why Thomas chose Tyrwhitt as a friend remains a mystery for he was known as a disreputable individual. The saying is that opposites attract each other.

Before setting out on the journey Tyrwhitt persuaded Thomas to sign a document stating that if either died during the journey the survivor would be heir to the property of the other.

On 27 September 1738 the two men were drinking together in a tavern in Montpellier, France. While Thomas enjoyed himself greatly Tyrwhitt could only think of the document. He plied Thomas with drink and when the latter was quite inebriated he provoked him into a duel. Tyrwhitt, contrary to Thomas, had been drinking at a slow pace. Thus when Tyrwhitt took on Thomas he was sober. Thomas was no match. Tyrwhitt killed his friend that night. The corpse of the unfortunate Thomas was shipped to St. Donat's. Tyrwhitt spread the rumour that Thomas was killed by an unknown Frenchman.

The shock of Thomas' death would have provided his widow with a motive for a haunting. especially as his death has up to the present day remained somewhat of a mystery. Thomas may not have died at all. There is some evidence to suggest that the corpse may have been a look-alike. Thomas had lost the first finger of his left hand when he was a child. His former nurse swore that the corpse had five fingers on the left hand and could therefore not have been Thomas. Accordingly this, if true, would mean that Tyrwhitt provided the corpse of a stranger in order to be able to claim the inheritance. Was the real Thomas Stradling still alive?

While the spectre of Lady Stradling is sinister enough, there is an even more fearsome spectre around, the ghost of a hideous-looking witch. She can sometimes be seen in the Armoury.

Cat lovers will be delighted to learn that the castle is also the haunt of a phantom puss. If you expect a deep chesty purr from the spectral moggy you will be disappointed. All you will get is a soft growly rumble. The cat of St Donat's does not belong to the small domestic kind that is able to purr. On the contrary, the feline ghost is quite substantial. It is the ghost of a panther. The big phantom cat often pads leisurely along the castle's corridors.

It has been rumoured that the black cat also wears boots. On the other hand some researchers have suggested that fact and fiction became muddled up and that mythology has entered reality. The story of 'Puss in Boots' comes to mind. A little humour is needed in a sad business.

In one of the bedrooms of St Donat's Castle, bright, luminous spectral eyes sometimes spy on the sleepers.

Swansea
The Wailing Ghost of Pennard Castle

The legend of Pennard Castle Castle in Swansea includes elements of mythology. Two of the supernatural occurrences linked with the castle are not, strictly speaking, true ghost phenomena because they are caused by entities that cannot be classified as spirits of deceased people or beings. One of them is a fairy haunting. In traditional lore fairies are not ghosts but a living race of flesh and blood.

The second haunting is caused by a *gwrach-y-rhibyn*. The *gwrach-y-rhibyn* is quite similar in nature to the Irish *banshee*. The *banshee* in turn belongs to the fairy race. It follows that the *gwrach-y-rhibyn* can therefore be quite safely grouped with the fairies. The *gwrach-y-rhibyn* does consequently not cause the same type of haunting as a ghost, simply because the *gwrach-y-rhibyn* is counted as a living creature whereas a ghost belongs to the realms of the dead.

The area around the castle is also troubled by a true haunting, the ghost of a wailing woman. Legend has it that the woman haunts the castle and the surrounding region because she was unable to get over the death of her lover. When the woman found out that her lover had been killed she committed suicide. Her ghost returned from the grave to haunt the castle and its surroundings.

Numerous witnesses have experienced the haunting. In the 1970s the wailing ghost even appeared to a whole group of students who were camping near the castle. During the night they were awoken by the piercing screeching of a woman. The screeching seemed to come from the nearby castle. Eventually, two young men made for the castle to explore the area. On their way up an invisible presence passed one of the explorers on the narrow path. He clearly felt the ghostly being as it squeezed past him. Despite the uncanny incident they proceeded to the castle and had a good look around. They found the ruins and the surrounding area completely deserted. Then the two young men returned to the camp.

In the meantime the students in the camp kept an eye on the castle. All of a sudden the bright moonlight revealed a dark and mysterious shape in the ruins of the castle. After a while the strange entity left the castle and made its way down the path. At this point the students in the camp became rather worried, for if the strange creature stayed on the course it had taken it was inevitably going to bump into their two friends. They decided to send out two men to warn their friends. The two parties met up eventually and compared their experiences.

It appears that the two explorers really had a brush with the dark shape from the castle. The students in the camp saw the strange creature walking towards them and, indeed, one of the explorers noticed an invisible presence passing by.

Swansea

The White Lady of Oystermouth Castle

Can you spare a minute of your time? If so, reserve that precious moment for the White Lady of Oystermouth Castle in Swansea. She needs our love and comfort. Spend a few minutes with her and she may feel inclined to tell you what really happened to her many years ago.

The White Lady of Oystermouth Castle has been seen on numerous occasions in and around the castle. She often appears behind a tree crying in distress or walking through the outer wall of the castle. Some witnesses noticed that the back of her white dress is torn and the flesh beneath raw and injured. The White Lady is presumably a victim of immense torture. The injuries on her back stem, with a great degree of certainty, from a punitive beating. The lady in the white dress was most likely a prisoner who was whipped to death on the castle's whipping post. This infamous post has survived the centuries and can still be seen nowadays. Her presence seems to frighten animals. A witness related that the White Lady scared his dog exceedingly.

Another witness, Peter, drove past the castle on a rainy Wednesday night in March 2003. Suddenly he spotted a woman in a white dress on the battlements. He could clearly see that the woman needed help so he stopped the car and walked up to the castle. As Peter drew nearer the woman turned around and showed him her back. He was shocked to see that the dress was torn and that the woman's back was raw and bleeding. The first thought that came to his mind was that the poor woman was a victim of crime. Peter was even more determined to help her but when he reached the gate of the castle he found it locked. He called out loudly in order to attract the woman's attention but she did not appear to hear him. Peter was both amazed and frightened when the lady in white vanished before his eyes.

Welshpool *(Trallwng)*, Powys
A Spectral Piano Concert at Powis Castle

The old castle in Welshpool has a talented tenant, a musician. Off and on his lithe fingers pass over the keys of the piano in the ballroom and the whole room fills with beautiful music. He is a bit like Erik in 'The Phantom of the Opera'. Nobody has ever seen him but he is undoubtedly always present.

Spooky events have been witnessed around the Ballroom Wing of the castle. The piano frequently begins to play when the ballroom is locked and therefore devoid of any human presence. When checked the room always turns out to be empty. On one occasion the piano stool had been moved from its original location. These incidents may be connected with some ghostly entity that has been heard leaving and entering the ballroom.

What does one do if a completely unknown woman dressed in outlandish clothes all of a sudden enters one's bedroom and sits down on the bed to have a rest? The building supervisor of Powis Castle and his wife are often confronted with this question. The shade of a woman with old-fashioned headgear on her head frequently manifests herself in their bedroom, which is located near the ballroom. Her activity consists of sitting on the bed.

What tragedy lies behind the death of the child who apparently loved to wear green garb? The spirit of the child can sometimes be seen in the castle. The child ghost still has a preference for green. It is also known that the phantom has long hair.

There is nothing better than a warm log fire on a cold and rainy day. The lady in black who often sits in a chair beside the fireplace in the Duke's Room seems to love a roaring fire.

Is that also the reason why she has come back from the realm of the dead to haunt this particular room? Some ghosts remain earth-bound because they enjoyed living in a certain location so much. Was the room with its warm fire her version of paradise on earth? Is there any connection between the lady in black and the phantom woman who has been spotted near the door of the Duke's Room.

The woman near the door may just be part of the hazy shapeless crowd that haunts the gallery leading to the Duke's Room.

Powis Castle has its very own hound-haunting. The spectral dog that inhabits the old kitchen area cannot compete with the hound of Baskerville Hall. It is a sad trapped animal that desperately tries to leave the kitchen. The dog has so far been heard, but never seen. It sounds as if the ghost of the animal were trying to break out of the kitchen.

The spectral inhabitants of Powis Castle generate a high noise level. They knock on doors and windows and the echo of phantom footsteps reverberates in the corridors. Sometimes they even touch visitors with invisible hands.

3

Haunted sacred buildings

Generally speaking churches, abbeys, cathedrals, monasteries and priories are places of refuge where the worshippers can find peace and shelter from worldly worries. One can indeed find peace within the walls of these buildings but sometimes one may also find that they have worries of their own. These are not always small inconvenient everyday problems like, maybe, the lack of funds.

The sacred and majestic edifices have seen torture, treason and murder. Torture most commonly took place in the form of immuring. Accordingly, skeletal remains were found behind the walls of Monkton Old Hall and Brecon Cathedral. A monk of Neath Abbey betrayed Edward II to his enemies, and murders were committed in Ewenny Priory and Titern Abbey. Quite often the victims of the crimes return from the grave to haunt the places of their suffering. But it is not always a crime that is at the centre of a haunting. The ghost of Cardiff Cathedral has its roots in an accident and St. John's Church and Usk Priory are haunted because of broken promises.

Brecon *(Aberhonddu)*, Powys
The skeletons of Brecon Cathedral
One should expect to rub shoulders with a ghost or two in a building as old as Brecon Cathedral. The site was sacred even before the present building was constructed on it. It was

sacred to the druids who performed their healing rites in the area where the cathedral now stands. But even the history of the present building looks back on many centuries.

The cathedral started its life as a Norman Benedictine priory in 1093. After the dissolution of the monasteries the priory became the Parish Church of St. John the Evangelist. When the diocese of Swansea and Brecon was created in 1923 the church became a cathedral.

Over the centuries legends were woven around the building. One of them is the legend of the nuns that were immured alive within the walls of the cathedral. It is said that the skeletons of the unfortunate nuns were found when some walls were broken down in the cathedral. The saying is that the ghosts of the nuns have returned from the realms of the dead to haunt the site of their cruel death.

Cardiff
She still visits Cardiff Cathedral
It is thought that the ghost of a woman haunts Cardiff Cathedral and the area around the nearby river. She is still looking for her young son who went missing a long time ago. The mystery that surrounds the disappearance of the boy has never been solved. He could have just run away or else he could have been murdered. The most likely solution is that he drowned in the Taff.

Ebbw Vale *(Glynebwy)*, Blaenau Gwent
The forlorn lady of St. John's Church
Like many old buildings St John's in Ebbw Vale has a ghost. A young woman with dark hair haunts the surrounding area and the remains of the church. The woman holds a baby in her arms. She particularly haunts the banks of a nearby stream, from where she makes her way to the church. She vanishes as soon as she reaches the church gate. According to

legend she committed suicide. Here, then, is what happened to her.

In the nineteenth century a woman had an affair with a young man called William who was the son of a wealthy landowner. William returned her feelings and therefore the scene seemed to be set for a happy end. Unfortunately, William's father had other plans. William had already been singled out as a bridegroom for the daughter of his father's best friend. William soon learned about the marriage arrangement. If he had been honourable he would have stood by his beloved fiancée but the young man had other plans. Fully aware that he was never going to marry the love of his life he at least wanted to enjoy the last remaining days with her. This was contrary to the lady's wishes. She would not have a sexual relationship with William without marriage.

He resorted to an almost Shakespearean trick to have his way with the unsuspecting woman. William openly told her about his father's plans and that he would be disinherited if he disobeyed. He therefore suggested a secret marriage, which the woman gladly accepted. The ceremony went ahead but it was not legally binding. One of William's friends impersonated a minister and wed the couple. Some time after the 'wedding' William told the young woman the truth. He rudely dismissed her, telling her that his real marriage was imminent. By then the woman was already pregnant, but not even that could alter William's mind. The woman never recovered from the shock. She gave birth to the baby but after that her courage failed her and she committed suicide by throwing herself in the stream near the church, together with her baby.

The story ends with poetic justice. About nine months later William accidentally drowned in the same stream. He left behind a bride who found herself in the same situation as the young woman a few months before – she had given birth to a baby and William was gone.

According to another version William was solely responsible for the tragic events. In this account his father did not interfere with the relationship. Like in the previous tale the young woman refused to give herself to William without a proper marriage. Here again William arranged a bogus ceremony and deserted the bride in much the same way as in the other version. He told the woman the truth and informed her that he was planning to get married for real to another woman. By then the woman was already pregnant. William's father was not at all pleased with his son's behaviour. He basically ordered his son to marry the young woman legally. William refused, whereupon his father disowned him. The young woman lived long enough to hear of William's real wedding – and to give birth to her child. In the end, just like in the previous story, she took her baby and threw herself in the stream near the church where she drowned. William suffered the same fate: a few months later he accidentally fell in the stream and drowned.

Ewenny *(Ewenni)*, Vale of Glamorgan
Ewens returns to Ewenny Priory
Ewenny Priory, now in ruins, was founded by Maurice de Londres in 1141. Since then the venerable walls of the fortified priory have seen innumerable holy services. Sadly, there were also a number of not-so-holy events that occurred in the priory.

The ancient building was once the site of a murder. Ewens, a monk of the priory, was killed by a Norman baron. Murder is one of the common causes for a haunting. Accordingly, the ghost of the monk now often appears in the ruins.

Murder is always a horrifying act and Ewens has our sympathies. While nothing can justify murder the fate of Ewens is at least known and he can thus be mourned and remembered properly. This does not hold true in the case of the young child dressed in blue clothes whose ghost has been seen wandering around forlornly in the ruins of the priory. The child's identity has remained unknown to this day. It is not known what fateful events surround the history of the child in blue.

Haverfordwest, Pembrokeshire
A meeting with a monk at Haverfordwest Priory
The priory was founded around 1200 by the Agustinians. Since then many centuries have passed leaving their scars on the walls of the priory. Although the building is now in an advanced state of decay the monks have stubbornly refused to abandon it. Perhaps they are somewhat spectral now. But that is not surprising at all because the saying is that the building has been haunted for centuries. Sometimes the phantom monks show themselves to passers-by.

Early in the morning on a sombre winter day Martha and Edith passed the priory on their way to work. Suddenly a spectral monk materialised in the gate of the ruined building. He wore a habit with a hood shading his face. The monk spotted Martha and Edith and decided to approach them. As he drew nearer he signalled to the two witnesses to join him by crooking his finger. At that point the monk's hood fell back and the two ladies noted that the phantom had dark eyes. The ghostly monk was apparently quite eager to make contact with the two women for he came closer still. The thought of a close encounter with a phantom was too much for the two ladies. Edith fainted with shock and Martha ran away screaming. Somewhat later Martha was able to muster enough courage to return to the priory to help her friend. By the time she reached Edith the latter had already come round again.

The encounter with the ghost left the two women too shaken to go to work that day.

Llangollen, Denbighshire
The singing monk of Valle Crucis Abbey

A ghostly monk sometimes visits the Valle Crucis Abbey in the Vale of the Cross at Llangollen.

The earliest recorded sighting of the monk goes back to the days when horse-drawn carts still dominated the roads. In those days two churchmen travelled through the Vale in the early morning hours. They were on their way to see another clergyman. When the two churchmen reached the ruins of the abbey they saw the shadowy figure of a monk, who sang beautifully in Latin. They decided not to disturb the monk and listened quietly to the singing. The two clergymen were completely unaware of the passage of time. When the singing came to an end the day had fully broken. The churchmen were upset when they realised that they had missed the cart that was to take them to their final destination by about three hours. Little did they know then that the incident saved them from injury or death. The cart was involved in an accident and one of the passengers was killed.

The singing was heard in more recent days. A lady from Liverpool passed by the abbey in 1950 and heard a choir singing to the accompaniment of an organ. She was in the company of a friend who was unable to hear the music. The lady from Liverpool somehow felt that some tragedy had happened in the abbey.

On another occasion a man heard the singing. As in the previous case his friend could not hear the voice at all.

A lady from Wrexham and her aunt had an even more startling experience. One night they came near the ruins of the abbey and saw the ground in front of the abbey bathed in brilliant light. They also saw a high golden statue and several persons all dressed in gold. All of them wore golden helmets. Suffice it to say that like in the other cases the aunt was not aware of anything. The spectacle finished abruptly. No singing was heard.

Llangynwyd, Bridgend
Anne's return to Llangynwyd Church

The ghost of Anne Thomas is said to haunt Llangynwyd Church. The haunting has its origin in a local romantic tale from the eighteenth century.

Ann Thomas who lived with her parents at Cefn Ydfa lodge was in love with William Hopkins, a thatcher and poet from Llangynwyd. Ann's family was against the relationship and forced her to marry Anthony Maddocks, a wealthy gentleman from the village. Anne continued to love William and died two years after the marriage of a broken heart. William Hopkins never married and survived Anne by only fourteen years. He died in 1741 at the age of forty. Anne and William are both buried at Llangynwyd Church.

Anne's spirit is restless. It is believed that she has returned from the grave to search for her lost love.

Margam, Neath
'Tom of the Fair Lies' haunts Margam Abbey

Wealth can buy a lot of things but it cannot buy happiness or a life free of calamities. Margam Abbey was born rich. Robert, Earl of Gloucester, gave the abbey 18000 acres of land which provided it with a lucrative income. Margam was in fact the richest abbey in Wales.

Despite its wealth, the abbey did not always have a carefree life. An uprising of lay-brothers in 1206 was probably the most serious crisis in the abbey's long history. The lay-brothers occupied the dormitory and took control of the food supply. They also chased away the abbot and assaulted the cellarer. The rebellion was eventually put down and the lay-brothers were severely punished.

The haunting of Margam Abbey may partially have its origin in the rebellion of the lay-brothers. Their act of disobedience may have caused a haunting. The ghosts of several deceased monks occasionally manifest themselves in the grounds of the building. They may be the ghosts of the rebellious lay-brothers.

Amongst Margam's many ghosts there is a local celebrity, the ghost of a Cistercian monk. Local legend has it that the ghost was once 'Twm Celwydd Teg' *(Tom of the Fair Lies)*. Far from being a liar, his name was a metaphor for his ability to predict the future.

Twm once told a nest robber that he was going to die within three days and that he had better be careful if he wanted to avoid an untimely death. The ruthless nest robber had little time for Twm and went about his heartless business as usual. Three days after the warning the man climbed on a high tree to plunder the nest of a kite. As he reached for the eggs he got bitten by a viper which the parent bird had left in the nest for the chicks. Completely in shock, the man fell from the tree and broke his neck.

The saying is that time is a great healer. We heal as we forget. Unfortunately, time is indiscriminate. It blurs all memories. Often we would like to retrieve lost memories only to discover that this is not within the limits of our abilities. Time is stronger than our feeble attempts to dig in the past. Accordingly, the well-dressed and apparently wealthy gentleman who occasionally manifests himself in the abbey has become a faint echo in history. He has a story to tell, but our ears are deafened by the passage of time.

Monkton
The skeleton of Monkton Old Hall
Old Hall in Monkton is thought to be the haunt of a spectral nun. It was founded in 1098 and was once part of a priory. The building is therefore likely to have picked up the ghost of a cleric here and there.

A former occupant of the building, a Rev. Tudor Evans,

reported to a local newspaper that he had heard heavy knocks on his bedroom door for several nights in a row. The noise always stopped as soon as his foot touched the floor. Nonetheless the reverend would still answer the door. However, each time he found the area in front of the door deserted. The reverend also peered down the corridor and would therefore have seen any retreating caller. But to his great surprise there was nobody there.

The family's daughter saw an eerie glow radiating from a room through chinks in the door when she was standing on the landing outside the room. She opened the door and looking into the room she saw a cowled apparition whose head and shoulders were leaning out of a window. The cowled ghost seemed to wave at somebody. After this incident the room was referred to as the Haunted Room.

The family dog felt comfortable anywhere in the building with the exception of the Haunted Room which he refused to enter.

A friend of the family once slept in the Haunted Room and promptly had an encounter with the ghost. He heard the rustling of long robes around his bed throughout the night. The witness was unable to light a candle for the flame was always snuffed out before it even reached the wick of the candle.

There is a convincing reason for the haunting. When repair works were carried out in the Church of St. Nicolas, the bones of a kneeling woman were found immured in the priest's room. It is also known that an old Benedictine priory was once attached to the church, of which Old Hall used to be a part. Researchers have speculated that the unfortunate person whose remains were found in a cavity of a wall in the priest's room was a nun who had committed an unpardonable sin. As a punishment she was immured. Her ghost now haunts Old Hall.

Neath *(Nedd)*
The treacherous monk of Neath Abbey
Maybe King Edward II should not have put all his trust in the monks of Neath Abbey, for after all one of them betrayed him to his enemies. But it seems that treason and being an informer never pays off in the end. The gain seems great when the evil deed is done, but it always comes at a small cost. The treacherous monk has never found any rest. He was expelled from the abbey as a punishment for the treason he had committed and thus condemned to lead a restless life. Even the tomb could not grant him any peace. When the moon is full the monk's ghost can be heard knocking on the building's door beseeching his brethren to readmit him to the abbey. This has always been the way with traitors: there is always a price to be paid. Many a passer-by has heard the sound of phantasmal knocking. Some say that it is indeed the spirit of the monk that knocks on the gates of the abbey. Others believe that it could be the ghost of King Edward II.

Pontrhydfendigaid, Ceredigion
Sisyphus of Strata Florida Abbey
During his lifetime he offended a god or two. Or was it that he always got the better of them that enraged the gods so much. Sure enough, the saying is that he kept Hades himself imprisoned and that the god of the underworld would have remained a captive indefinitely had not the war-like Ares rescued him. Ares gave him short shrift. The rogue, Sisyphus, was finally and to the great relief of the Olympians, thrown into the Tartarus. The gods had not heard the last of him. Sisyphus cheated Persphone and escaped from the clutches of the Tartarus. The story goes that it took Thesus to put an end to Sisyphus's career as a cheat and robber of unsuspecting travellers. Be it as it may, Sisyphus did finally end up in the Tartarus where an extremely severe punishment was imposed

on him. He was condemned to roll a black boulder up the brow of a hill and cast it down on the other side. So far Sisyphus has not been successful. As soon as he is within the reach of the summit the great weight of the boulder becomes too much for him and it slips out of his hands and rolls down to the bottom of the hill. Sisyphus is then forced to start his task afresh.

The abbey of Strata Florida in Pontrhydfendigaid was founded in 1164 and has fallen into a hopeless state of disrepair over the centuries. The monks of Strata Florida have not entirely given up on their abbey, at least one of them. It is said that he returns to the abbey every year on 25 December and attempts to rebuilt the abbey's altar. Like Sisyphus, the monk does not seem to be able to complete his task. Is the sheer interminable reconstruction of the altar perhaps a punishment imposed on him for some wrong he committed in the distant past?

Penmon, Anglesey
Every night at Twenty Past Two at Penmon Priory

A spectral nun is thought to haunt Penmon Priory. The phantasmal nun has appeared to a good number of residents. One of them is a curate who used to live with his family in the priory from 1947 to 1950. He never really saw the nun but he sensed her. A threatening presence used to wake him up every night at 2.20 a.m. The rest of the family did not seem to notice the supernatural occurrences in the priory. The curate felt the haunting much stronger when he was alone in the house.

A family father had a brush with the phantom nun when he visited the priory in 1980. The building was then open to the public. One evening near nightfall he and his family were approaching the priory when he clearly saw a nun looking at him from the distance. After a few seconds she walked into the priory. When he mentioned the incident to his family he found out that they had not noticed the nun. They decided to follow the nun into the priory. The building turned out to be completely deserted. There was no trace of the nun.

Prestatyn, Denbighshire
The nun in the window of Talacre Abbey
No! An emphatic no! The abbey is definitely not haunted. Those who live around the abbey maintain that it is a lovely place which is not haunted at all. They claim that the frequent reports of spectral activity in the building are damaging the image of the abbey and that of the nuns who once occupied it. The strong denial of the locals does not explain away the experience three children had over a decade ago.

In 1994 three children who were playing in the grounds of the abbey saw a ghostly nun when they looked up to one of the windows. The unearthly pallor of the nun's face frightened the children. They knew all at once that they had seen a ghost. When they mentioned the incident to their parents they were told that the nuns had long since left the abbey.

Psychic researchers have recorded spectral voices in the surrounding area of the chapel. There maybe a possible connection between the voices and the dark, spooky shadows that have been seen wandering past one of the chapel's gates. Soon after those ghostly beings had been sighted the door started to swing on its hinges without any visible source that could have caused the movement. The candles in the chapel were also affected by the haunting; they went out one after the other.

Swansea
Who haunts Rhosili Rectory?
Rhosili Rectory is located in a lonely spot, midway between Rhosili and Llangenith on the Gower peninsula. The loneliness around the building may well have had a rôle in the

creation of the numerous ghost stories connected with the rectory and the surrounding area. The rectory also has a long-standing connection with death. An excavation revealed that the site was once occupied by a church. It follows that there must have been a churchyard. Some of the ghosts may have their origin in the former churchyard.

Two of the rectory's former occupants, a reverend and his wife, experienced a haunting. A man and a woman appeared to them. The reverend placed the ghosts in the Edwardian period because of the way they were dressed. Both reverend and wife must have been quite frightened when the ghosts moved so close to them that they were only a few centimetres away. They could therefore give a good description of what they had seen. The reverend clearly noticed that the skin of the ghosts had the greyish colour of elephant skin. He also believed that the structure of the skin was like elephant skin. One could hold against this that the reverend was unlikely to have been an authority on elephants, least of all an authority on their biological make-up. In all probability the reverend and his wife saw two ghosts whose skin was affected by the taint of decomposition. This interpretation would create a link with the church discovered in an excavation in 1979. The haunting could have originated in the churchyard.

The mysterious phantom who frequently manifests itself behind the occupants of the building saying, 'Why don't you turn around and look at me?' is probably one of the ghosts from the Edwardian period. Be it as it may, this theory yet needs to be confirmed as so far no-one has had the courage to turn round. Who then is the frightening entity that haunts Rhosili Rectory?

Some of the former residents of the rectory complained about a ghost that creeps out of the ocean at night and enters the building. This creature has not actually been seen. Only its presence has been felt. Is it the ghost of a victim whose life was claimed by the sea, some unhappy soul that drowned and returns from depth of the ocean?

The spectre of the Reverend John Ponsonby Lucas haunts the surrounding area of the house. He does in death what he used to do when he was still alive, which is riding up and down the beach. As his parish was rather spread out the reverend spent a considerable time of his life on horseback in order to meet his parishioners.

Tenby *(Dinbych-y-Pysgod)*, Pembrokeshire
The phantom priest of St Mary's Church

Everybody should be welcome in the house of god. The phantasmal priest who haunts St Mary's Church seems to be of a different opinion. For whatever reason he makes visitors feel unwelcome.

Several visitors have felt strange and uncomfortable in the sacristy of St Mary's in Tenby. This feeling is thought to be caused by the ghost of a priest who frequently appears in a corner of the church. The phantom priest only stays long enough to allow the witnesses to catch a fleeting glimpse of his presence. Sometimes he has been seen walking down the aisle.

The priest does not belong to a recent century. His style of dress reveals that he was alive during the Reformation.

Tintern *(Tyndyrn)*, Monmouthshire
The shy monk of Tintern Abbey

A spectral hooded monk often shows himself in Tintern Abbey, near Chepstow. The ghost likes to walk around in the ruins. Sometimes the monk can be seen on his knees praying beside one of the arches in the western part of the abbey. Some visitors attempted to speak with the monk, which disturbed or frightened him. Instead of giving a response he disappeared. Perhaps he is of a timid nature. Is the shy monk also part of the invisible choir of monks whose beautiful chanting can sometimes be heard in the abbey?

A Saxon warrior carrying an arsenal of weapons around with him roams through the building off and on. Some time ago a couple of tourists claimed that they enabled the warrior to pass on by saying a mass. How effective their exorcism was remains to be seen.

Who defiled the sacred space of the abbey with foul murder so many years ago? It is thought that a woman was murdered within the walls of the abbey at some stage in the past. Her ghost has returned from the world beyond to point an accusing finger at her murderer.

Usk *(Brynbuga)*, Monmouthshire
The Spectral Nuns of Usk Priory
The saying is that the Benedictine priory of Usk has been haunted for many centuries. It is believed that five spectral nuns haunt the building. The phantom nuns sometimes appear to visitors.

A woman who visited the priory in 1970 saw five ghosts. Unsurprisingly they were the spectres of nuns. They manifested themselves near the library and walked over to the church. It is of significance that exactly five ghosts seem to haunt the priory. When the monasteries were suppressed five nuns then resident at the priory were given a pension. They were also made to swear an oath of allegiance to the king. Complying with the king's wishes undoubtedly saved the nuns' lives. Yet, it remains to be asked whether they were able to live on happily after the dissolution of their priory and, especially, after swearing an oath to the king. When they were admitted to the order the nuns swore an oath to serve God alone, and swearing a special oath to another master must have seemed to them like a violation of their original vows. There is also the matter of the acceptance of a pension. The pension came from secular sources, which meant that the nuns were suddenly in the pay of a secular authority. This meant that they had practically retired from serving their God. They had a different paymaster. The severe violation of their vows and the spiritual treason must have left the nuns in a state of despair and discontent. The nuns thus had a good motive to return from the realm of the dead.

4

Haunted private and public buildings

The most widely-known ghost stories are connected with castles and sacred buildings. We come across these stories mainly in books and films. The hauntings in these buildings do not affect us: on the contrary, they amuse and entertain us. This creates the impression that a haunting always strikes miles away from everyday life. The truth is far more uncomfortable. The majority of the supernatural occurrences in the world take place in private homes and public buildings. A ghost can trouble us in the warmth and safety of our own house. Phantasmal footsteps in the room upstairs or rattling chains in the hallway are not unusual. In extreme cases there may even be a Grim Reaper sitting on one's favourite chair. All these incidents seem to be within the limits of one's imagination. It becomes more complicated when ghosts takes up residence in unromantic locations like power stations or universities. Exactly this happened at the Caerleon Campus at the University of Wales College in Newport, the Wylfa power station, and many other public buildings.

Aberaeron, Ceredigion
Murder in Aberaeron
Llania House in Aberaeron was once the property of a sailor. It is known that the seaman owned the house in 1790 and that he was married with two sons.

The elder brother followed the family tradition and became a sailor like his father, whereas the younger brother was afraid of the sea. The idea of dying at sea and a subsequent sea burial, the cold and watery grave, was the prime cause of the young man's fear of the sea. The elder brother was married; nonetheless, this did not keep him at home. He continued with his seafaring.

One night, when the sailor was on one of his sea journeys, his brother merrily chatted with his sister-in-law and innocently kept her company. The sailor unexpectedly returned that night. As he passed by a well-lit window he could see his wife joyously engaged in a conversation with a male stranger who he could not identify through the window. Believing that he had been cuckolded the sailor flew into a terrible rage and rushed in with his sword drawn. The sword came down on his young wife and decapitated her. When the sailor came to his senses he realised that it was only his harmless brother who had been speaking with his wife. The young woman's head began to haunt the house.

In another account the sailor killed both his wife and his brother, whereupon the young woman's head started to trouble the building.

The brother was buried in a cemetery near the sea. In time his fears were realised. While he was alive he avoided travelling by sea for fear of dying during the journey and the subsequent sea burial, but in death the sea began to eat away at the cemetery and one day the man's grave slid into the sea. His ghost returned from the watery grave to trouble Llania House.

The saying is that even nowadays the spectre of a man in dripping wet clothes sometimes appears in the building. It is also believed that the spirit of the murdered woman is still restless. Her head appears unexpectedly floating in mid-air for a while.

Aberystwyth, Ceredigion
The Jewel Lady of Nanteos Mansion

It is thought that the ghost of Elizabeth Powell roams the corridors of Nanteos Mansion near Aberystwyth searching for her lost jewellery.

Elizabeth was the wife of William Powell, who had Nanteos Mansion built in 1738. She is known as the Jewel Lady. Elizabeth hid her jewellery in a safe hiding place before her death. Legend has it that her spectre still haunts the hallways in search of her lost gems.

A phantom coach and a phantasmal horseman often appear in the area around Nanteos Mansion. It is said that the spectral vehicle drives up to the main entrance at night. The coach and its horses are clearly visible whereas the haunting of the horseman can only be heard.

Legend has it that a ghostly lady with a lit candle on a candlestick sometimes visits the staircase of the building. Her appearance heralds the death of a member of the Powell family.

Off and on the enchanting melodies played on a harp resound in the mansion. It is known that the almost magical hands of the harper Gruffydd Evans weave these tunes on an ancient harp but it is somewhat difficult to watch him at work. The harper never shows himself. Gruffydd Evans is a ghost.

Spectral visitors seem to feel rather comfortable at Nanteos Mansion. Apart from the ghosts already mentioned there are a famous Grey Lady, a whistling servant boy in the hallways, a ghostly furniture remover and a haunting in the Pink Room!

Argoed, Caerphilly
The ghost house of Gwent

Some years ago the Wards rented a council house in Argoed which had no known record of supernatural occurrences. The situation changed with the arrival of the Wards. The family began to be plagued by inexplicable noises. Shuffling footsteps, sighs, blurred images of people, moans and raps on the walls frightened the family exceedingly. The haunting made Mrs Ward mentally ill. She was admitted to a psychiatric hospital where she stayed for about two months.

In the meantime Mr Ward and the children went through a period of sheer horror as the haunting became even more intense. The ghosts were now clearly visible. On one occasion Mr Ward saw the ghostly body of a man resting on one of the beds. The house ceased to be of any practical use to the family. They only dared to stay there during the day. Friends offered them shelter for the night.

The police aided by psychic researchers investigated the occurrences in the house. They concluded that the disturbances were not caused by human activity.

Because of the intensity of the haunting the house came to be known as 'The Ghost House of Gwent'.

Beaumaris *(Biwmaris)*, Anglesey
Ghost or vampire?

It is believed that Baron Hall in Beaumaris is haunted, although the exact nature of the apparition has so far not been defined clearly. Some witnesses even claim that the mysterious being that has taken up residence in Baron Hall is a vampire

Baron Hall is situated about six miles outside Beaumaris and can be reached only by using lonely long and winding lanes. The isolated location of Baron Hall and its derelict state probably contribute much to the vampire legend. Be it as it may, the rumour of a vampire-haunting rather than a ghost-haunting continues to circulate in Beaumaris. Nobody dares to go near the old building at night.

Is there any evidence that could have given rise to the

belief of a vampire haunting? Maybe. The grounds of Baron Hall house an ancient family tomb. A flight of overgrown stairs lead downwards to an iron gate with bars in its upper part that allow visitors to peer inside. The tomb stores six ancient coffins. The existence of the spooky tomb is almost like a chapter taken from Bram Stoker's *Dracula*.

In the light of another theory a ghost-haunting appears to be more likely. Baron Hall is far away from any church in the neighbourhood. The absence of any sacred buildings throws up the question whether the grounds of the tomb have ever been consecrated. Burials in unconsecrated soil have often been given as a reason for the return of spirits.

Beaumaris, Anglesey
The death of Richard Rowlands
Beaumaris Gaol looks back on a short but violent history. It was built in 1829 by Joseph Aloysius Hansom who is also the inventor of the Hansom Cab. The gaol was closed in 1878 and subsequently became a police station. The building currently serves as a museum.

During its relatively short life as a gaol the building was the scene of innumerable acts of violence. Many inmates of the prison were sent to the whipping room, where they were shackled to the whipping frame to be whipped with a lash. The gaol also had a gruesome gibbet which must have filled the prisoners with indescribable terror. Richard Rowlands was led to that gibbet and publicly hanged for the murder of his father-in-law. He always maintained that he had not committed the crime. Most likely he went to his death as an innocent man.

The great suffering of the prisoners is in all probability the source of the haunting of Beaumaris Gaol. It is tempting to connect at least some of the supernatural occurrences with the death of the unfortunate Richard Rowlands. His death is shrouded in mysterious events. On his way to the gallows Rowlands predicted that the four faces of the nearby church clock would never show the same time again. Rowlands prediction was correct. For a long time the clock behaved as foretold by Rowlands.

Innumerable phantom noises haunt the building. These noises include ghostly footsteps, rattling keys, banging and creaking doors, to name but a few.

Some of the supernatural phenomena are of a more violent nature. Some witnesses have reported being physically attacked by an invisible presence. It is thought that the attacks are carried out by the shadowy shapes that often appear in the corridors of the building.

Beddgelert, Gwynedd
She wears a long red silk dress
Living economically sometimes comes at a small cost. Money is saved on one side, but a payment in kind has to be made on the other side.

The Newmans lived in Craflwyn Hall in Beddgelert from around 1960 to 1994. During that period they closed up part of the building to cut down the maintenance costs. Immediately after the alterations in the building the family began to hear noises in the closed-up part every night. The Newmans lacked courage to investigate.

One day Mrs Newman fell asleep on a chair in the kitchen. When she awoke she saw a beautiful woman in a long dress of red silk standing beside her. Mrs Newman recognised the Red Lady at once, for she had seen a portrait of her. The lady in red was Mrs Parry. She also knew that the Parrys were former owners of Craflwyn Hall and that they had long since passed away.

The National Trust bought the mansion in 1994. While the building was being restored a volunteer from the National

Trust lived and slept in the kitchen. He complained about an atmosphere of malevolence in every part of the mansion and also confirmed the presence of the uncanny noises.

Brynford *(Brynffordd)*, Flintshire
No changes, please

The ghost of the founder of Llwynerddyn Hall in Brynford has returned to his former property.

In 1973 the Oldham family owned Llwynerddyn Hall. The family felt that the building was due to be renovated. As soon as the renovation work began the ghost of a man dressed in Elizabethan fashion appeared. He is believed to be the founder of the house. It appears that the phantom did not like the changes in the building.

On one occasion Mrs Oldham saw the phantom from the Elizabethan era sitting on a chair at the top of the stairs. The ghost looked like a person of flesh and blood. The apparition was so real that Mrs Oldham was even able to judge the mood of the ghost. She described the ghost as contemplative. Mrs Oldham had many more encounters with the ghost. When she worked on the floor upstairs the phantom appeared and walked through a wall. The ghost chose a spot in the wall where a door used to be.

Cardiff
They removed his ashes

Dunbar Smith designed the National Museum of Wales in Cardiff and it was consequently built according to his instructions. Smith saw the building in its finished state and lived happily ever after and that should have been the end of it all. Unfortunately, life is not always as simple as that.

After Dunbar's death the urn with his ashes was kept in the central block of the museum. Some years ago the urn was moved to another location. It now rests near the gents' toilet.

Dunbar seems to dislike the new location. He probably thinks that it is not very dignified to be kept near a toilet. Dunbar began to voice his opinion strongly. He started to haunt the building. At first he concentrated only on turning on electrical equipment. After a while this did not seem enough and he appeared in person.

One night an attendant was doing his rounds in the museum when of a sudden he felt followed by somebody. He turned around and noticed a tall, gaunt man in black clothes. The stranger was looking at the display cases. The man in black vanished before the attendant's eyes.

Cardiff
The phantom of the New Theatre
Phantoms of the opera certainly exist. The New Theatre in Cardiff has a story to tell.

The spectre that haunts the New Theatre is not quite as impressive as Erik *(The Phantom of the Opera)*, nor does the phantom being have Erik's musical talents. All this pompous and fancy phantom behaviour cannot be expected from an elderly lady. Nature has not endowed her with a beautiful singing voice. But, Erik, you know what? She has a quality that matters more than all the beautiful music you produced. The elderly lady is kind and benevolent.

The elderly woman often appears in one of the boxes where she seems to look for something. From there she walks down the stairs to the stalls where she suddenly disappears. The haunting is thought to have its origin in the death of a woman who died when she fell from the box she now haunts. In an alternative version the elderly lady was found dead in the building after the matinee performance. Be it as it may, the ghost is benevolent and even helpful. On one occasion the ghost saved the life of an electrician who was fixing a spotlight. He lost his balance and would have fallen had not some invisible force caught hold of his leg to pull him back. When he turned round to thank his rescuer he realised that there was nobody around.

Cardiff
The Museum of Welsh Life and its ghosts
The Museum of Welsh Life in Cardiff houses a number of buildings collected from all over Wales. These buildings were taken apart and reassembled on the grounds of St. Fagan's Castle. The collection of historic houses include workshops, cottages, farms, a school and a chapel. It appears that some of the former tenants have even moved with the building substance. Some of the buildings are haunted.

It is known that Llainfadyn Cottage was built in 1762, for the date when the first stone was laid is carved on the right hand side of the fireplace lintel. The small cottage offered a confined space in which the occupants had to live. If there is nothing much available one has to be inventive. In order to grant the individual members of the family some privacy furniture was used to separate the beds from the living space and the hayloft was reserved for the children. Although many decades have passed since the cottage was built some of the children are still around. Both staff and visitors alike have seen phantom children playing in the building.

Llainfadyn Cottage would have been the home of people who did not own enough land to live off. These people would have been farm servants and craftsmen or, in the case of Llainfadyn Cottage, quarrymen and their families.

The situation of Cilwent Farm was somewhat different. The occupants seem to have been much better off. The building even had its own dairy. In architectural terms Cilwent Farm is a long house. This means that cattle and humans lived together in the building separated only by a door. The animals were housed at one end of the building and the farmer and his family at the other. Some of the occupants still show themselves in the farmhouse. Now and again footprints appear out of nowhere in the dust on the floor of the building.

It is thought that the ghost of Lady Plymouth often appears in 'The Arts And Crafts Italian Garden And Nurseries' and leaves a strong scent of perfume behind. It is also known that the ghost of a young female gardener keeps returning to the building.

St. Fagan's Castle was once the property of the Earls of Plymouth. It is said that one of the earls was poisoned and that his disembodied voice can at times be heard crying, 'Sarah, Sarah'.

The castle is also full of inexplicable noises like ghostly voices that address the workforce by name, and the singing of Welsh tunes, as well as phantom footsteps.

Some of the beams in the roof of Penrhiw Chapel once served as biers on which corpses were carried to the graveyard. In and around the chapel a spectral funeral procession often appears to the visitors. This funeral procession is considered an omen of death.

Cilcain
A lady, a hunter, a horse and a pot of spicy stew
Brithdir Mawr is situated on the lower slopes of Moel Famau near an ancient track in the vicinity of Cilcain. It was built in the fourteenth century. The building has retained most of its original features.

A house so steeped in history should also have its share of ghosts. One of them is a lady in a blue dress from the middle ages. A wimple covers her head. The lady in blue likes to appear in the master bedroom.

A married woman woke up one night to see the lady in blue standing near her sleeping husband. After a short while the phantom lady turned round and walked away from the bed. She made for a wall where she traversed a walled-up door.

The ghost of a medieval huntsman has been seen repeatedly around Brithdir Mawr. The spectral hunter was spotted in 1920 and again in 1958. He always appears in company of a ghost horse. Mounted on his ghostly companion the hunter can be seen riding along the ancient track near Brithdir Mawr.

The building is also haunted by a phantom scent. The nature of the scent has been described as pleasant. It is reminiscent of the smell of spicy stew simmering on a stove.

Conwy
Mr Jones of Aberconwy House
Aberconwy House in Conwy was built in the fourteenth century. Despite its great age parts of the original building have survived the erosive power of time, as have some of its former inhabitants.

Sometimes the ghost of a Victorian gentleman appears in one of the corridors. It is believed that this is the ghost of Mr Jones who lived with his much younger wife in Aberconwy House between 1850 and 1880. Mr Jones died the day his seventh child was born. It is thought that the coincidence of birth and death is a strong enough cause for a haunting. When the moment of death arrived Mr Jones must have been especially distressed when he realised that he was not going to see the new-born child growing up. The sorrow Mr Jones felt may have caused him to return from the grave. Occasionally Mr Jones also appears in one of the ground floor rooms.

The first owner of Aberconwy House was Evan David. The ghost of his wife is said to haunt the area near the fireplace in the loft. Her presence is linked with a phantom smell of flowers. Sometimes she can be a bit physical. She likes to touch those who have the courage to enter her domain.

The ghosts of Aberconwy House have a wicked sense of humour. They like to hide objects in the house and wake up the occupants with loud footsteps at night.

Conwy
Where is Dr Dick?
Plas Mawr, built in the sixteenth century, was once the home of Sir Robert Gwynne and his family. A fatal accident occurred at Plas Mawr while Sir Robert was abroad. His pregnant wife fell down a steep flight of stairs, dragging with her their three-year-old son. The accident left mother and child gravely ill. Servants laid them in the Lantern Room and sent for a doctor. The doctor arrived after a short while. His name was recorded as Dr Dick. The doctor realised at once that mother and son were fatally injured. There was nothing he could do to rescue them. At this point the story becomes confusing. It has never been convincingly explained why the elderly housekeeper locked up Dr Dick in the Lantern Room.

The accident coincided with Sir Robert's return to Plas Mawr. He found both wife and son dead when he entered the Lantern Room. There was no trace of Dr Dick. Although his patients were already beyond rescue when he arrived at Plas Mawr the doctor presumbly thought he would be blamed for their death. It is believed that Dr Dick consequently attempted to escape from the room by way of the chimney which joined with others and also with passages in the walls. Up he climbed driven by fear and desperation until he lost his way in the maze or died from the noxious fumes of the house's fires. It is said that the doctor's ghost began to haunt the labyrinth of the chimneys and indeed spooky sounds sometimes emanate from this area.

Legend has it that Sir Robert committed suicide in the room where his family had died. His ghost now haunts the Lantern Room where he appears as a dark figure.

Gwernymynydd, Mold, Flintshire
The crone of Tŷ Gwernen

Tŷ Gwernen is situated in Gwernymynydd in the vicinity of Mold. The romantically located building, which stands on a hill, is the scene of a haunting.

Paul Matthews was peacefully resting in his bed when he suddenly noticed the face of an old crone staring at him through the window. He clearly saw her face and described it as extremely ugly and repulsive. After a few seconds the old woman vanished into thin air.

Paul's younger brother John is also aware of the ghost. He once had a brush with the phantom crone. One evening John was watching TV when the old woman walked in. The ghost did not seem to take any notice of John. She walked over to the fireplace where she remained for a while looking at the wall. Then she disappeared before John's eyes. He noted that the spectre was very old. Her hair was white and her face thin and pinched. The encounter with the ghost frightened John so much that he sheltered in the kitchen for the rest of the night.

The crone also troubled Nathan, Paul's older brother. Although Nathan could not see her he was still aware of her presence because he could hear her tapping and scratching in his bedroom.

While Nathan was unable to see the ghost of the old woman he clearly caught sight of another ghost. One night on his way back home from the Swan Inn Nathan witnessed a haunting on the lonely road that links Tŷ Gwernen with Gwernymynydd village. He noticed a tall shape swaying along the road some distance in front of him. Nathan could not quite make out what or who it was. He only noted that the apparition was unnaturally tall and swaying like a drunken man.

The haunting of Tŷ Gwernen has been attributed to an incident in the 1890s. At that time an old woman lived in Tŷ

Gwernen. It is known that she had a mentally handicapped son. In those days it was considered shameful to have a mentally disabled person in the family, and quite often they were hidden away. The old woman's son was no exception: he was kept like a prisoner and never allowed out. One day he turned on his mother and strangled her.

Laugharne *(Lacharn)*, Pembrokeshire
The ghost of a poet?

The poet Dylan Thomas used to live in the house called the Boathouse in Laugharne. The saying is that he has never completely left the building. It is believed that the poet's ghost haunts the Boathouse. The haunting was noticed for the first time in 1958 and still continues in our time and age.

The haunting of the Boathouse is slightly controversial. Some researchers have concluded that the poet is not involved in the haunting. They believe that the spectre of his mother causes the supernatural events in the building. An invisible force often moves objects like chairs and books around. Dylan's mother spent a few years in the house as a tenant. It could therefore be argued that her ghost has returned to haunt her former home. This theory has a weak spot; nobody has ever noticed a female ghost in the Boathouse.

Many locals believe that the poet himself is behind the haunting. There is substantial evidence to support this assumption. Dylan's ghost has been seen roaming the lanes in the vicinity of the house.

Llanbadrig, Monmouthshire
The phantom of the opera and the power station

It is thought that the ghost of Rosina Buckman haunts the ground around Wylfa power station near Llanbadrig. Rosina was born in New Zealand. She was already a famous opera singer when she moved to the UK at the beginning of the twentieth century.

In the 1930s Rosina bought a holiday house on Wylfa Head. The house was named Galan Ddu. Descriptions of Rosina's appearance still survive in the area. She used to wear white gowns and was often seen with her pet dog, a Pekinese. It is known that Rosina and her husband were extremely happy at Galan Ddu. She was forced to sell the house during the Second World War because the RAF needed the ground.

The ghost of Rosina Buckman was first seen in August 1964 during the construction of Wylfa Nuclear Power Station near Cemaes Bay. Workmen from the night shift saw the phantom when they were excavating a tunnel. From then on the ghost appeared frequently. The spectre is always dressed in white. Rosina wanders around happily humming melodies. Her happiness may well be the cause of the haunting. It has been argued that Rosina was so happy at Galan Ddu that she has no need to move on. Galan Ddu is her idea of paradise.

Some researchers believe, however, that Rosina's ghost is searching for the lost ashes of her mother-in-law. Rosina's mother-in-law, Emma d'Oisley, loved Galan Ddu and visited it often. Emma died in 1935. Her body was cremated and the ashes were interred at Galan Ddu. When the power station was built Emma's ashes were removed and buried at Llanbadrig Church.

Llandeilo, Carmarthenshire
The tragic life of Elinir Cavendish
Newton House was the scene of tragic events that resulted in a murder. Legend has it that the spirit of the victim returned from the realm beyond to haunt the building. A phantasmal lady in a white dress frequently shows herself in the house. The beautiful lady in white was once Elinir Cavendish.

At the beginning of the eighteenth century Elinir Cavendish ran away from an arranged marriage. She found shelter with her relatives at Newton House in Llandeilo.

Elinir's fiancé caught up with her and murdered her in the building. The ghost of the unfortunate woman began to haunt Newton House.

In the 1980s when Newton House was owned by a television facilities company Elinir showed herself frequently. One evening the director and an editor noticed the ghost of a young woman in one of the rooms. The phantom glided across the room and walked into a cupboard. They searched the cupboard immediately and were greatly surprised to learn that the woman had gone.

The employees of the company complained about a strange atmosphere in the house and quite a number of them even fell ill.

It appears that there are also numerous male ghosts. Nobody has ever seen them. They always remain invisible. Only the sound of muffled disembodied masculine voices reveals their presence. Pipe and cigar smoke can sometimes be noticed even if nobody smokes. The smoke and the male voices my be linked.

Llanelli, Carmarthenshire
Suicide or murder?

Llanelly House was built by Thomas Stepney in 1714. At a later stage the impressive house in Llanelli was split in two halves. Each half was owned by a doctor of medicine. One of them was Dr Thomas Beddlington Cook.

A maidservant, Mira Turner, fell in love with Dr Beddlington Cook's son and became pregnant by him. Pregnancy without being married was considered shameful and dishonourable during Mira's days. Women who became pregnant outside marriage were shunned by society. Rather than face such a fate Mira committed suicide. The saying is that Mira took an overdose of laudanum and that as a result of this she fell down the stairs, causing her death. Her death certificate gives her death as suicide.

Did Mira really commit suicide? The circumstances of her death appear to be somewhat strange. An overdose of laudanum seems credible enough as a cause of death. On the other hand the fall down the stairs on top of the laudanum poisoning has a taste of incongruity. Was she murdered and if so by whom? Dr Beddlington Cook's son, as the illicit father of Mira's child would have had a motive. If he had been outed as the father of Mira's child he too would have been shunned by society. Did he murder Mira to cover up the illicit relationship?

Be it as it may, Mira's ghost now haunts Llanelly House. She often shows herself on the stairs that played a role in her death. Sometimes only the phantom sound of a long dress dragging on the floorboards reveals the presence of the spook.

Llanfihangel Crucornau, Monmouthshire
Open questions

When the clock chimes midnight and the last stroke is sounded the old day dies and a new one begins. For a split second it is neither today nor tomorrow. It is thought that the barriers between our world and the world of the dead open during such transitional periods. Ghosts can then travel quite freely from one world to another.

The lady in white who haunts Llanvihangel Court in Llanfihangel Crucornau makes efficient use of this rift between the worlds. She appears in the building with the twelfth stroke of the clock. The lady in white always leaves Llanvihangel Court and makes for a nearby stretch of woodland which is called Lady Wood. The name of the woodland probably has some connection with the fate of the White Lady. Was she murdered in Lady Wood?

There is substantial evidence to support the theory of a murder. A skeleton with a bullet lodged between its ribs was found in the area around the building a few decades ago. Were those the remains of the White Lady?

On one occasion a former owner of Llanvihangel Court heard the ghostly screams of a woman coming from Lady Wood. Did he hear the death screams of the White Lady?

Legend has it that once a sword fight took place on the stairs. Swords were crossed and some fighters fell wounded or dying. Their bleeding bodies are thought to have left three indelible bloodstains on the stairs. Was the fight the prelude to the death of the lady in white? Did she escape from the melée hoping to find safety in Lady Wood? Did one of the combatants pursue and kill her? Did he subsequently bury her where the skeleton was found?

The ghost of a little green-eyed man occasionally appears in the White Room of Llanvihangel Court. Is there a link between the green-eyed man and the White Lady. Was he her murderer?

Llangathen, Carmarthenshire
The fearsome ghost of Aberglasney House

Aberglasney House was built in Llangathen in the seventeenth century. Around 1630 five maidservants died from the noxious fumes of a stove while they were asleep in the Blue Room. Their death was announced to the housekeeper by the appearance of five corpse candles. According to legend the candles have kept appearing ever since that tragic event to foreshadow another death.

The spirit of Thomas Phillips who once owned the building returns at regular intervals to his former home. He also shows himself in the surrounding area of the house. Since his death in 1824 a large number of people have seen the ghost of Thomas Phillips.

A former head gardener of Aberglasney House, Joseph Hallet, was well aware of the haunting. He often warned, when the night had fallen, 'He's about tonight'. Hallet claimed to have had an encounter with the ghost of Aberglasney in 1912.

Although Hallet did not refer to the ghost by name in his famous lines he most likely meant the spectre of Thomas Phillips.

On the same note, it was probably also Phillips who terrified the German prisoners in their sleeping quarters when Aberglasney House was used as a POW camp during World War I.

Years later the phantom man showed himself to Kate, a maidservant at Aberglasney House. One night the presence of the ghost scared the young woman so much that she left her bed and fled from the house. Kate found shelter in her grandmother's cottage, where she explained that the phantom had even pulled the blankets from her bed.

A particularly violent incident occurred near the end of World War II. One night a burly lorry driver with tattoos all over his body and rings in his ears called in to see his girlfriend, who was a maidservant at Aberglasney. He mocked the ghost and called up the stairway challenging the phantom to show itself. The spectre answered with a blood-curdling screech and sent a howling gust of wind down the stairwell. The lorry driver panicked and stormed out of the house. He started up his lorry and fled. He never challenged the ghost of Aberglasney again.

Llangollen, Denbighshire
The Ladies of Llangollen

When the famous Ladies of Llangollen, Lady Eleanor Butler and Sahara Ponsonby, owned Plas Newydd in the early years of the nineteenth century it was a hub of academic and social events. Their education and great hospitality won them a large circle of friends and acquaintances. Celebrities like the Duke of Wellington were among the friends of the ladies.

Dr Mary Gordon, a Jungian scholar, spent some time at Plas Newydd in 1930 and felt the spetral presence of the two

166

women. Dr Gordon returned to Plas Newydd some months later and actually met the ghosts of the two ladies when she walked down the Bache. It is said that the two ladies were sitting on a bench in the sunlight. Sarah and Eleanor had an almost inseparable link with the Bache; it used to be their favourite walk.

Dr Gordon had the presence of mind to address the ghosts. A meeting at Plas Newydd was agreed upon. She was to meet the two ghosts at nine o'clock that night in the building. The ghosts kept their promise and Dr Gordon wrote a book about the meeting. It transpires that the two ladies decided remain earth-bound because they were so happy at Plas Newydd.

Mold, Flintshire
The ghost of Bailey Hill
At the foot of Bailey Hill in Mold stand four terraced Victorian houses. They look pleasant in their idyllic surrounding. On a bright sunny day one may feel tempted to go for a walk on a route past the four house and up on the hill. But there are rumours. It is said that one does well to avoid the four houses after sunset. The locals believe that the houses are uncanny. They are haunted.

A young woman once stayed in a room at No. 4 which in Victorian days belonged to a maidservant. During the night she noticed a presence in the room and her bed began to shake. It is said that the windows of this particular room do not remain closed.

Several years ago a man had a brush with the haunting when he stayed in the former maidservant's room. During the night loud knocking on the window awakened him. Of a sudden the ghost threw open the windows. The man also caught a glimpse of a figure walking downstairs.

The master bedroom is the most haunted room in the

building. One night the owner of the house woke up because she felt somebody pushing against her left side. A ghost tried to dislodge her from her bed. She was little inclined to give up her bed to a phantom and held against the pressure. When this did not produce the desired result she began to pray. After a while the pressure ceased but the ghost was still on the offensive. The spectre seized the owner by the shoulders and tried to pull her out of the bed. Suddenly the uncanny visitor groaned loudly and let go of its victim and a small black blob rolled away from the bed towards the fireplace where it vanished.

The phantom blob is not the only ghost in the room. On another occasion the owner woke up because somebody jabbed a finger in her ribs. A young spectral woman with ginger hair sat beside her on the bed and giggled happily. The owner decided to ignore the ghostly woman, for she seemed harmless enough. After some time the ginger-haired phantom dematerialised.

Sometimes the ghosts of No. 4 visit the house next door. A man with a cap often walks through one of the walls in No. 4 and enters the bedroom of the neighbouring house. The building adjacent to No. 4 has its own ghosts. The spectre of an old woman in a night dress, glasses and a mob cap appears in one of the bedrooms.

Monmouth *(Trefynwy)*
He saw his father
Lower Bailey Pit in Monmouth, once a farm, is thought to be the most haunted house in Monmouth.

It is known that a man with a wooden leg used to live in the building. The man's ghost began to haunt the house after his death. The clattering of his wooden leg can still be heard as the phantom walks up and down the stairs.

Legend has it that a maidservant was murdered on the

stairs leading down into the cellar. Even now the screams of the unfortunate woman sometimes reverberate in the cellar area. When Lower Bailey Pit was still a farm an employee heard the phantom screams and was so frightened that he handed in his notice immediately.

In more recent days a plumber carried out some repair work in the house and heard a door slam shut. At first he paid little heed to the incident and simply opened the door again. A little while later the door was slammed shut again. The plumber knew for sure that he was all by himself in the house. He therefore concluded that no earthly hand had shut the door. The thought of sharing the house with a phantom frightened him so exceedingly that he departed instantly.

In 1970 a group of men who were fully aware of the building's reputation decided to hold a seance in it. The atmosphere was inspirational. It was a rainy and spooky night. Almost as soon as the men had made themselves comfortable in the house they began to hear noises and footsteps in the rooms above them. One of the man, John, seemed to have had a gut-feeling that the haunting was anything but benevolent. He therefore urged the group to leave immediately. They ran out and gathered on the driveway.

John's brother David soon recovered from the shock and decided to go back in to explore the house. When the rest of the group had worked up enough courage to follow David the latter was a good bit ahead of them. He was already on the stairs and made for the upstairs rooms. David shouted over his shoulder that he had seen his father upstairs and was all eager to meet him. The uncanny bit was that David's father had died when he was a baby. A split second later David changed his tune, and greatly scared, he shouted that something was coming after him. His friends shone their torches up the stairs and sure enough they saw the stairs behind David bending under an invisible weight. The invisible presence also raised clouds of dust. By then David had disappeared in the upstairs part. The men followed him and found him almost frightened out of his wits in one of the bedrooms. At the same time every single member of the group sensed an all-permeating presence of evil in the building. They felt that it would have been unwise to leave the room. Consequently, they decided to stay in the room for as long as necessary. John came up with the idea to sing religious tunes to ward off the evil ghost. They sang 'Bread of Heaven' and after some time the malevolent presence withdrew. The men then hastily made their way out of the building.

There are versions of the incident that mention a follow-up in which only David was involved. Despite the terrifying haunting he had experienced in the building David still believed that he had seen his father that night. The saying is that he returned to Lower Bailey Pit and that he did not leave it alive.

In summer 1993 Lower Bailey Pit was destroyed in a conflagration. It has been rebuilt since. It is rumoured that the site is still haunted.

Mynydd Isa, Flintshire
A spectral pet

Imagine you are at home and you call for your dog. You expect to see your dog within a few seconds, but an unknown dog appears to answer your call. Impossible! This is exactly what Mr Emery thought until he learned one fine day that there are more things between heaven and earth than we can even dream of.

A phantom dog often shows itself in Primrose Cottage in Mynydd Isa. Mr Emery first noticed the canine spectre when he heard the footsteps of a dog on the stairs. Believing it was his own dog Misty he called for the animal to come back. Mrs Emery told her husband that Misty was not upstairs but right beside him. At this point the family realised that their home was haunted by a phantasmal dog. The spectral animal sometimes even walks straight through the living room.

Quite often the dog is in the company of a human ghost. The shape of the human apparition is so indistinct that it cannot be clearly ascertained whether it is an old man or an old woman.

Spectral visitors seem to feel at home in Primrose Cottage. Occasionally a tall phantom man in a grey sweater makes himself comfortable in the kitchen area.

At times the ghosts can be a bit mischievous. On one occasion when Mr Emery was on the phone one of the ghosts pinched him. Despite their impish nature the ghosts support and protect the family most of the time. One particular ghost warns the occupants of accidents with a whistling sound.

When the Emery family took over Primrose Cottage much restoration work had to be done. Mrs Emery's brother volunteered to help with the repair work. One day when he was drilling into a wall he heard a whistling sound. A second later he hit a wire and got an electric shock. It appears that one of the ghosts made an attempt to warn Mrs Emery's brother of the imminent danger.

Nelson, Caerphilly
An atmosphere of doom

Llancaiach Fawr Manor in Nelson is an ancient building. It was built in 1530. It is known that a much older house occupied the site before the manor was built. Over the centuries a host of ghosts have made Llancaiach Fawr Manor their home.

It is said that two phantom children haunt the grand staircase. The spectral children show themselves occasionally. Most of the time they prefer to remain invisible but their voices can still be heard. The two children are harmless and do not trouble the residents. This cannot be said of some of the other infant ghosts that appear in the manor. They scare the residents by touching them.

The spectre of Mattie, who was a servant, often shows herself in the kitchen. As in bygone days Mattie can be seen baking bread. She also feels drawn to her former bedroom on the upper floor. Mattie always remains invisible in the bedroom but her presence can still be felt. She announces her arrival by creating an atmosphere of gloom in the room. Most occupants of the bedroom complained about being affected by a feeling of deep sadness, which they attributed to the presence of Mattie.

While it can be an unpleasant experience to meet the ghost of Mattie nobody has ever complained about Colonel Pritchard. The colonel owned the manor in the middle of the seventeenth century. One should have thought that he has long since left but he is still around. Off and on he roams through the building dressed in a colourful uniform.

The ghosts of Llancaiach Fawr Manor generate a lot of noise and tricks of light and shadow. Visitors must be able to cope with disembodied voices, spooky shadows, and faces that appear suddenly on the walls.

Newbridge, Caerphilly
The haunted landing

Celynen Collieries Institute and Memorial Hall in Newbridge is more widely referred to as 'The Memo'. It was built in 1898 to provide the community with a working men's club. The building had a sizeable library, billiards room, committee room and reading room. The Memorial Hall was added in 1924 in remembrance of the soldiers who died in the First World War. It was equipped with a number of entertainment facilities which included a cinema, a stage, and a dance hall.

In the 1980s the building was closed and soon fell into

disrepair. Liam and his girlfriend Bethan founded a group called 'Friends of Newbridge Memo' in order to save the building. The group managed to raise some considerable funding which was used for restoration work.

One evening Liam, after working in the building, locked up and did his rounds. When he was climbing the stairs that lead to the dance hall he saw a woman standing on the landing near the library. She was dressed in the style of the 1940s. Of a sudden the woman vanished into thin air.

The woman from the 1940s is not the only spectre in the building. A phantom usherette frequently shows herself in the old cinema.

Newport, Monmouthshire
'Big Bertha'

Bertha Ramsey, was nicknamed 'Big Bertha' because of her stately height. She was about 6 ft tall. At the time of her tragic end she was a matron at the Caerleon Campus at the University of Wales College in Newport. In 1962 Bertha was found dead at the bottom of a flight of stairs. It could not be established whether she fell or whether she was pushed. Bertha has not completely left the college. Her ghost still walks through the corridors. It is also believed that she operates the lifts in the college during the dark hours.

The University College was built on an ancient Roman burial ground. The desecration of the ancient tombs may have angered some of the occupants. A phantasmal Roman centurion in full armour sometimes shows himself in the building.

It may be worth a thought to introduce a Parapsychology course into the curriculum with all those ghosts walking around freely on the college campus!

Ogmore Vale, Bridgend
A Message from the other side

A certain house in Alma Terrace in Ogmore Vale has been the scene of a haunting for many decades. Lloyd experienced the ghost from childhood onwards. He lived in that particular house from the 1940s to the early 1960s.

It is believed that the cause of the haunting was the tragic death of a male tenant. The saying is that he took his own life by poisoning himself with gas. He died in one of the rooms in the house.

In 1956 when Lloyd was about eight years of age he slept in a haunted bedroom. One morning he woke up and noticed a tall white shape in his room. He was too terrified to scream. On another occasion ghostly hands stroked his hair. Once a spectral voice even mentioned to Lloyd that there was a ghost in the house.

His brother occupied that particular bedroom before Lloyd was born. He too was a victim of the haunting.

Lloyd was particularly scared of the kitchen because a sinister atmosphere permeated the kitchen area. He would therefore never stay on his own in the kitchen if it could be avoided.

It is thought that a member of the family became part of the haunting. One night Lloyd's aunt Nia and his parents went down to the Corbett Arms where they had a few drinks and a pleasant conversation. During the conversation the topic of life after death was brought up. Nia promised that she would give Lloyd's parents a message from the world beyond if anything happened to her. She died six months later.

A few weeks after her death the cracking sound of a whip awakened Lloyd's parents around 11 at night. The father explored the bedroom but could not locate the source of the noise. Thereafter he searched every part of the house. When he reached the bathroom he noticed that the bathroom light had come on and that water was pouring into the toilet bowl because the cistern handle was moving of its own accord. Quite shocked, he returned to the bedroom and told his wife about the strange incident in the bathroom. The wife believed that Nia was behind the strange occurrences. When the couple began to discussed her theory the cracking sound ceased.

Pembroke
Judge Meyrick of Bush House
The locals say that John Meyrick was a wicked man, a harsh and unrelenting man of the law. Perhaps he should never have been made the Chief Justice of South Wales. Even in death the judge has remained troublesome. His ghost stayed behind at Bush House near Pembroke, the judge's former home.

Meyrick's ghost has the appearance of an elderly man. The phantom shows itself mostly at night. Why the judge began to haunt Bush House is entirely open to speculation. It is thought that Meyrick's spirit became restless because his corpse disappeared under mysterious circumstances. Did the locals hate the merciless judge so much that they desecrated his body and dumped it somewhere in the wilderness? When alive he was powerful and untouchable. It was a completely different matter when Meyrick was dead. Maybe the place is just generally haunted and everybody who dies in the building becomes part of the haunting. There is some evidence to support this theory.

Three Irish workmen had several encounters with the ghost of a lady in a white dress in 1955. The Irishmen were employed to carry out repair work on Bush House. They were supposed to stay at the house for the whole period of the repair work. Accordingly the three men were given a bedroom in the building, in which they soon began to feel uncomfortable. The three men noticed a sharp drop of temperature in their room during the night. There was also knocking and rapping all over the room. The youngest of them had his overcoat pulled away which he used as a bedcover. That was the state of affairs after the first night. As a result of this the men refused to sleep in that bedroom. They were promptly moved to a bedroom on the top floor of the house. The room proved to be as haunted as their former room. From the window they could see a ghostly lady in white walking in the moonshine. The phantom lady frightened the three men so much that they escaped from Bush House and refused to sleep there ever again.

The building is also haunted by the ghost of a gentleman of medium built. He wears breeches, leggings and a worn shooting jacket. He usually carries a shotgun with two barrels. The gentleman is accompanied by three dogs.

One evening a night watchman had an encounter with this ghost. He was patrolling the building when he saw the spectre. At first the watchman was not aware that he had met a ghost because the man in the haunting outfit looked real enough. He spoke to the huntsman but got no reply. The ghost simply walked away and disappeared into a pond.

The haunting of the ghost in hunting gear is thought to go back to an incident in the nineteenth century. It is said that a gentleman who fits the description of the ghost lived at Bush House in those days. Legend has it that he went out hunting one day. As usual he was accompanied by his three dogs. He also carried the doubled-barrelled shotgun the watchman saw.

While he was out hunting he had a chance encounter with his wife, who was travelling back from Pembroke in her coach. When she saw her husband she pulled by and opened the door to speak with him. Just as she opened the door the huntsman's shotgun went off by accident and the pellets hit her. The injuries were fatal. The gentleman never recovered from the tragic death of his wife.

Pontblyddyn, Flintshire
Witchmarks

Plas Teg in Pontblyddyn was once the home of John and Margaret Trevor. It was built in 1610 and seems to have had an association with ghostly phenomena from the very beginning.

At some stage in the very distant past witchmarks were scratched in the main fireplace. In those days witchmarks were used to keep evil at bay. The marks can still be seen.

There was a good reason for the use of the witchmarks. Even when Plas Teg was only newly built it was already considered haunted. John Trevor's gamekeeper had an encounter with a ghost which frightened him so much that he commited suicide. Apart from the gamekeeper at least three other residents died of unnatural causes in the building.

The above figure does not include the victims of Judge Jeffries, the 'Hanging Judge', who lived in Plas Teg for some years. The evil judge used to hold court in the dining room of the building. His victims were then led to an adjacent room where they were executed instantly.

It is thought that John Trevor's daughter Dorothy died in an accident. The tragic events that led to her accidental death have made her spirit restless. The young lady's ghost began to haunt Plas Teg. The phantom lady has been described as rather pretty and blond.

Legend has it that Dorothy was forced to marry a wealthy squire whom she did not love. Her heart could not have been in that arranged marriage, because she was in love with Iorwerth, the son of a farmer who lived in the vicinity. Dorothy planned to run away with her true love. In order to provide materially for the relationship she decided to hide her jewels in a well so that she could easily take them with her on the day of the imminent elopement. Unfortunately, she lost her balance and fell into the well where she drowned. After her tragic death she began to haunt Plas Teg.

One of the bedrooms is particularly haunted. It is said that a threatening atmosphere emanates from it. A man who stayed in the room for a few nights described the atmosphere as sinister. He never felt comfortable in the room. When Miss Trevor finally materialised in his bedroom and sat down on his bed he was utterly shocked.

The haunting extends from the house to the surrounding area. Miss Trevor often shows herself on the road in front of the house. She appears so suddenly that she forces passing motorists to brake sharply. Some of the drivers were even convinced they had hit somebody and rang the police.

There is also an alternative version of Miss Trevor's death in which her lover died first. When the farmer's son learned that he has lost his great love because of an arranged marriage he hanged himself on the tree where the two lovers used to meet. Trevor's daughter subsequently died of grief. The ghosts of the two unhappy lovers returned to haunt the site of their suffering. They are also said to be the source of the phantom footsteps that can sometimes be heard in Plas Teg.

Several phantom riders occasionally appear in the area. The saying is that they patrol the area still doing what they used to do when they were alive, which was most likely to frighten poachers. They prefer to manifest themselves around dusk in the months of September and October.

The age of chivalry has not completely come to an end – at least not in the area around Plas Teg. A phantom knight in full armour often rides along the road near the building. Maybe he is still looking for some windmills to fight with in imitation of Don Quixote. In the modern age of wind-farms he may yet be lucky.

Pontypridd, Rhondda Cynon Taf
A cold hand was sliding down his back ...

The Municipal Hall in Pontypridd was once a Wesleyan chapel but fell into disuse in 1926. The council finally bought the building in 1956 and transformed it into a venue for events. It is said that there is a spooky atmosphere in the building.

Colin, who works in the building, witnessed the haunting on 30 May 1993 when he was tidying up the back of the stage. He was startled when he felt a cold hand sliding down his back. When Colin turned round he noticed a tall old man standing in the audience area. The slim and clean-shaven phantom wore an elegant raincoat and a suit. As the building was closed to the public at that time of the day the tall man should not have been standing there. Colin jumped off the stage and made his way towards the stranger. Before Colin could even utter a word the man vanished.

Port Einon, Swansea
John Lucas and his Merry Men

The Salt House in Port Einon was built in the sixteenth century. The founder of the house was David Lucas, who had it built for his son John. During its long history it has had numerous functions, one of which was the production of salt.

John Lucas was a fierce and violent man. He soon turned his home into a hideout for smugglers. While the authorities considered John a criminal the local people loved him, for he was somewhat of a Robin Hood figure. He freely shared his loot with the locals.

In 1703 a ferocious storm raged over the Gower area. The Salt House was flooded and struck by lightning. As a result of this a substantial part of the building collapsed. After that it was uninhabited until the nineteenth century, when cottages were built on its remains. The ruins of the cottages can still be seen nowadays.

It is said that the ghosts of the smugglers have returned to haunt the ruins of the Salt House, and that they can be heard carousing on stormy nights.

Porthcawl, Bridgend
The Maid of Sker

Legend has it that the ghost of Elizabeth Williams haunts Sker House. The phantom lady preferably materialises in one of the upstairs rooms where she was imprisoned for a while during her lifetime. The ghost's appearance is accompanied by the sound of clanking chains.

Isaac Williams had two daughters, Elizabeth and Mary. For many years they lived in Sker House in Porthcawl. Elizabeth was known as 'The Maid of Sker'. Her tragic history began when she went to a dance in the town hall of Kenfig where she met Thomas Evans. Thomas made his living in carpentry, but he was also an accomplished harpist. Elizabeth and Thomas immediately fell in love with each other.

Isaac Williams did not approve of the relationship because in his opinion Thomas was not his daughter's social equal: Williams was a gentleman farmer, whereas Thomas was a lowly carpenter.

The couple continued the relationship secretly. They knew that there was only one way open to them, which was to run away. One night Thomas arrived in a coach and waited for Elizabeth. Of a sudden the dogs of Sker House began to bark. The noise awakened the occupants and lights were lit in the building. Thomas thought it wise to retreat.

Mr Williams soon worked out what had happened that night. It is said that he imprisoned his daughter in her room to keep her from running away. Eventually Mr Williams arranged a marriage for Elizabeth. She got married to a Mr Kirkhouse from Neath. The saying is that her love for Thomas never died and that she pined for him all her life. She passed away nine years after her arranged marriage and was buried on 6 January 1710 in the churchyard of Llansamlet. Her tombstone was recently found in Llansamlet churchyard.

It is said that history has a way of distorting facts. There is evidence to suggest that Elizabeth actually lived a fulfilled and happy life. Mr Leslie Evans in his book 'Sker House' claims to have found two descendants of Elizabeth who are absolutely sure that she was happily married. If Elizabeth was happily married she would have had no obvious reason to haunt her former home. Who, then, is the ghost of Sker House?

It also appears that Thomas Evans was far from unhappy. He seems to have had a family with several children.

A phantom monk has been seen in the building. Upon closer inspection this is not surprising. The house was built by Neath Abbey in the twelfth century and served as a retreat centre for religious meditation. It is known that the monk was rather quarrelsome. He eventually fell out with his brethren and died an unnatural death. The monk's ghost groans in a frightening way and takes pleasure in scaring whoever he can get hold of.

Mumbles, Swansea
The blacksmith of Titchbourne Street
Around 300 years ago one particular house on Titchbourne Street in the picturesque area of Mumbles in Swansea was a village smithy. The blacksmith who once owned the smithy is still around but he has virtually faded away into invisibility. He is friendly but he can be a bit mischievous at times.

The spectral smith has so far remained invisible but everybody in the house knows that he is there. He makes his presence known in numerous ingenious ways. The ghost turns on electrical equipment and likes to throw the windows wide open. Sometimes phantasmal footsteps reverberate in the house.

The blacksmith has a mischievous kind of humour. A friend of the owner's daughter once stayed overnight. During the night she had a nightmare in which cold water was poured over her. She immediately woke up and found her bed soaked with water. On another occasion friends of the family kindly asked the ghost to switch on the TV. The spectre immediately turned it on.

The ghostly blacksmith is not bound to the house. He once followed the family to a DIY store and gave a clear sign of his presence. An invisible force knocked objects from a shelf when the family stood in front of it. The smith must have had a fantastic day out. A DIY store is just the place for a blacksmith to visit, even if he is a bit on the spectral side.

Pwllheli, Gwynedd
Thirst

In 1882 Mrs Greville Nugent went on a visit to Plas-yn-Rhiw in Rhiw to spend some time with her friend Lady Strickland.

One evening, after a long game of cards the two ladies decided to retire for the night around twelve o'clock. When they walked up the stairs which led to the bedrooms they noticed that somebody was following them. They knew well that the building should have been deserted so late at night.

The footsteps on the stairs were dragging and shuffling which conveyed the impression that they were caused by an old man. They also heard ragged breathing and coughing. When challenged the intruder did not reply. The uncanny stranger seemed to come nearer and nearer but inexplicably nobody could be seen on the stairs. In shock the two ladies held on to each other for comfort. They were paralysed with fear and could not move. The invisible ghost caught up with them and they could hear him passing the spot where they stood. The ghost dragged himself up the next set of stairs until finally his laboured breathing and coughing could no longer be heard. The two ladies decided to share a room for the night to have each other's protection.

Lady Strickland felt sure that the building was haunted. Out of interest she began to explore the identity of her uncanny resident. She made enquiries in the vicinity and found out that Plas-yn-Rhiw had once belonged to a squire with an enormous thirst for alcohol and that he drank himself into the grave. The assumption is that his desire for alcohol made his spirit restless.

Swansea
Olga
The ghost of a former patient haunts Cefn Coed Hospital. It is known that her name was Olga and that she suffered from paranoid schizophrenia. She was of small stature and had long ginger hair and large, green eyes. The unfortunate Olga committed suicide while she was a patient at the hospital. Olga is often taken for a living person because she looks so real. Olga loves singing, and quite like a living person answers when spoken to.

Once a member of staff, Helen, had an encounter with Olga. When Helen walked down one of the hospital's corridors she met a small woman with ginger hair and green eyes who sang in a strange language. The small woman stopped singing and asked Helen if she had come to punish her. Helen explained that it was not her intention to hurt her in any way whatsoever. Of a sudden the small woman walked away and disappeared into a nearby room.

Although Helen could not quite put her finger on it she felt a bit uncomfortable after the encounter with the strange little woman. She reported the incident to her manager. The manager was well aware of the haunting. He readily gave Helen the history of Olga.

Swansea
Just another nurse?
Half past four in the morning in 2003 is a moment in time that Frank will probably never forget. This is the moment when Frank, who works for Gorseinon Hospital in Swansea,

had an encounter with the supernatural. When he was washing his hands he looked up from the sink and noticed a strange-looking woman standing in the office door. The strange woman in her old-fashioned uniform was obviously a nurse, but nonetheless she looked totally out of place. Daniel also noticed that the nurse was not as physically solid as a normal human being should be. On the other hand she was not transparent either. Frank immediately went after her. The phantom woman made her way to the kitchen and from there she went straight to a cubicle. When the ghostly woman had reached the cubicle she vanished before Frank's eyes.

The presence of the phantom nurse appears to affect the hospital's equipment. A few years ago a member of staff shut down the ward for the night. As usual he also unplugged the radio in the kitchen. He was therefore quite surprised to hear the radio play loudly some time later. He returned to the kitchen to check on the radio and found out that it had been plugged in again. Later then he was amazed to learn that all the patients had been in bed and no member of staff had been anywhere near the kitchen when the radio began to play. The spectral nurse appears to have a liking for music.

Swansea
Jenny and the SS Titanic
A lady in a white dress sometimes wanders forlornly through the Grand Theatre in Swansea.

The lady in white is thought to be the ghost of a young actress who frequently performed at the theatre. Only her first name, Jenny, is known. She gave her last performance in Swansea in 1911. Straight afterwards she travelled to the United States – on the *SS Titanic!* Jenny was not among those who survived the catastrophe.

In 1972 an actress, Eileen Mason, had a brush with the spectral lady. While she was acting in *A Streetcar Named*

Desire she noticed an elegant lady in a dress of dazzling white colour. Of a sudden the lady vanished before her eyes. Ms Mason mentioned the incident to the manager who confessed that he too had seen the phantom.

The spectre also appeared during the performance of *Babes in the Wood*. The actress Irene Cooper was waiting all by herself in the wings to make her entrance unto the stage when she suddenly felt the touch of a cold hand on her shoulder. The touch of the phantom hand greatly frightened Ms Cooper.

Some researchers have suggested that the actress who died when the *Titanic* sank is not the cause of the haunting. They believe that the ghost in the white dress is the famous soprano Adelina Patti.

Swansea
The cellar of Swansea Museum
On October 31, 2007, just in time for the ghostly Halloween period, the *South Wales Evening Post* revealed that Swansea Museum is a haunted place. It is said that a number of female ghosts haunt the grand staircase and the landing. These ghosts come and go and have never been known to harm anybody. Well, but the cellar is a different story altogether. It is said that there is a malevolent presence in the cellar. It is thought that women notice the haunting of the cellar more than men.

Talacre
The phantom lighthouse-keeper
The ghost of a former lighthouse-keeper in an old-fashioned uniform still does his duty at Talacre Lighthouse. The phantom lighthouse-keeper has been seen going about his work as if he were still alive. He often appears to be fixing equipment in the top of the tower where he is easily visible even over a great distance.

The strange appearance of the keeper frequently inspires passers-by to explore the lighthouse. They invariably find it locked and chained up. Human presence in the tower is consequently unthinkable.

Two witnesses once wondered whether the tower was still in some way inhabited. One of them put it to the test and knocked on the door whereupon somebody inside the building answered 'Hello, who's there?'

One evening around 8 o'clock Mr Fox and a friend discovered a human footprint of colossal size near the lighthouse. Of a sudden there was a loud bang in the tower. The uncanny noise scared the two witnesses so much that they ran away. When they had run some distance they turned round to see whether they were being followed and noticed that somebody was shining a torch at them.

Talley *(Tallyllychau)*, Carmarthenshire
Buried face down

Mrs Williams worked as a servant at Talley House in Talley during the middle years of the twentieth century. Generally speaking she seems to have liked her time at Talley House, but one particular incident changed her attitude towards her workplace.

One day Mrs Williams had an encounter with a phantom man in a dark cloak when she entered a corridor in the building. The ghost approached her with a shuffling and limping gait. Mrs Williams backed away from the apparition. When the ghost kept advancing towards her she turned on her heels and made good her escape.

After that frightening incident she had no mind to return to the house but economic need compelled her not to hand in her notice. However, Mrs Williams worked up enough courage to relate the incident to her employer. She learned that every resident of the house was aware of the haunting. One of the owner's daughters was so terrified that she would not stay on her own in the house.

For a long time Mrs Williams hesitated to make her experience with the cloaked ghost known to the public. She finally came forward in 1966.

Researchers have thought of a possible connection between the haunting and the ruins of Talley Abbey. The ancient building of the abbey is close to Talley House and legend has it that the two sites are link by a subterranean passage. The haunting would then most likely be caused by a deceased monk. There is indeed some circumstancial evidence to support this theory.

Some time ago research workers investigated the remains of the abbey. One of the researchers that worked on the grounds of the abbey was Mrs William's brother. He dug up the skeleton of a man with his face buried downwards. In bygone days practitioners of magic were frequently buried in this fashion to keep them from returning from the dead. Is the occupant of the grave the cause of the haunting of Talley House?

Tongwynlais, Cardiff
The ghosts of Greenmeadow Mansion
There was once a majestic mansion that stood in Tongwynlais near Cardiff. This is the history of the Greenmeadow Mansion and the history of what happened to it when it had disappeared from the surface of this planet. Does it sound like a paradox, something is gone but yet it continues to add to its history? Know you not that there are things more powerful than time, things that are stronger than the impermanence of life?

In 1974 local newspapers reported that a council house on a site formerly occupied by Greenmeadow Mansion was haunted. Although there is almost nothing left of the original mansion, the ghosts may well have their origin in Greenmeadow.

In one of the houses on the council estate Mrs Davies and her children experienced a haunting in 1974. She repeatedly saw the spectre of an elderly woman in one of the upstairs bedrooms. One incident was particulary frightening. The ghost manifested on the landing and called for Mrs Davies's daughter June.

The Davieses were also troubled by loud banging noises and ghostly footsteps and the taps were turned on by some invisible force. Especially the phantom footsteps are of interest. Decades earlier a witness, Martha Moggridge, complained about a footstep haunting at Greenmeadow. This lends some support to the theory that the haunting in the modern building has its origin in Greenmeadow.

The *Cardiff Leader* finally investigated the haunting in the council house. A reporter, Bill Corke, and a photographer, Keith Baker, spent a night in a bedroom of the haunted part of the house. They too had an encounter with the ghost. Around 2 o'clock in the morning an eerie haze began to fill the bedroom. They also noted a drop in temperature.

Greenmeadow dates back to the seventeenth century, when it was owned by the Lewis family. The mansion was troubled by ghosts even at a comparatively early stage of its history. In 1860 the Melingriffith Band played at an annual supper organised by Henry Lewis. At the end of the event the band left. When the musicians were walking along the driveway of Greenmeadow a ghost appeared out of nowhere. The musicians were so frightened by the apparition that they dropped their instruments and ran away. They retrieved their instruments in broad daylight as they were too scared to return to Greenmeadow by night. It was not quite clear what the musicians had seen. They only said that the ghost was 'fierce, foul and awful'.

There was once a gardener at Greenmeadow, Daniel, who refused to let the children of the house play in a certain part of the garden. Gwen Wyndham Lewis, the daughter of Henry Lewis, explained that Daniel used to chase her and her friends out of the haunted part of the garden saying to them, 'Indeed to goodness keep away, will you'. Daniel himself only reluctantly worked in that part of the garden. It has always remained a mystery why the gardener was so scared of that section of the garden. One morning he was found dead in the mysterious part of the garden. Daniel's facial features were distorted with fear. The official version of his death stated that he had died of heart failure. In view of the fact that some of the Greenmeadow's dogs were found dead next to him it may be allowed to voice serious doubts as to the correctness of the cause of his death.

The Oak Room of former Greenmeadow was the most haunted room of the mansion. Two ghosts used to appear in this room. One was a red-haired man who appeared near a window leaning on his sword. He would suddenly kneel down as if to say a prayer. He always vanished soon after that.

In 1886 Captain Mostyn, a soldier who fought at Rorke's Drift, had an encounter with this ghost. He slept in the Oak Room and was awoken around dawn by three heavy knocks on the door. He looked up and saw a tall red-haired man leaning on a sword by the window looking out into the garden. Suddenly the ghost dropped his sword and fell on his knees. Then he began to pray. The ghost disappeared as abruptly as he had appeared. The Captain mentioned the incident to Henry Lewis and was told that the ghost of the red-haired man had been seen frequently.

Articles dealing with the haunting of Greenmeadow usually mention the Captain's encounter with the red-haired ghost as his main experience. However, a close look at a letter written by a Miss Moggridge, who was another witness of the haunting, reveals that Captain Mostyn also saw a small old man in old-fashioned clothes who was tapping on the walls of the Oak Room.

Gwen Wyndham Lewis names a number of witnesses who had experienced the haunting of the Oak Room. She mentioned a Miss Moggridge of Rhiwbeina, a doctor whose name she did not give, and Mary Anne Langley of Greenhill, Cardiff.

Gwen even informed the public about the haunting of Greenmeadow. She wrote to the *Cardiff Suburban News* and presented a letter which had been written by Miss Martha Moggridge. The letter was originally addressed to Gwen's father, Henry Lewis. In this letter she gives Henry Lewis a detailed account of her experience with a ghost in the Oak Room. In support of her witness statement Martha refers to Captain Mostyn's experience. The letter also reveals another detail about the Captain. It informs us that he served in the 24th Regiment.

In 1878 Miss Moggridge and her sister Mabel stayed at Greenmeadow for some time and were given the Oak Room. One night at exactly 3 o'clock they had an encounter with a ghost clad in a green coat with silver buttons, white knee breeches, lace at the wrists, and a silver rapier on a red sash. The sisters described the ghostly man as small and oldish, with a large nose and an abundance of white hair. The man in green simply flung open the door of the Oak Room, looked in, and entered. It appears that he was as surprised by the unexpected encounter as the two women for he passed his hand over his eyes in astonishment. This means that he must have noticed the two sisters. Yet he did not answer when Mabel addressed him asking him who he was. In fact, the man in green completely ignored them and made his way to one of the walls. Then he began tapping the wall a yard from the floor. After a while he threw up his arms in despair and vanished. At this point Miss Moggridge cited Captain Mostyn's experience with the haunting. Here she revealed that the Captain had also seen the small old man.

Martha's letter also refers to ghostly footsteps in the house. At one stage the footsteps were so frightening that the gamekeeper John Palmer was aroused and sent to investigate the cause of the footsteps, loaded gun in hand.

In connection with Greenmeadow the tragic fate of Kati Coch must be mentioned. It may well have influenced the haunting of Greenmeadow.

Around 1840 Kati, a young girl of Romany origin, was in love with a man who was nicknamed Magpie because of his style of dress. He always wore a black jacket and breeches, and a white waistcoat. Magpie was a tinker by trade and, unfortunately, not an honest man. He talked Kati into stealing silver from Greenmeadow which he sold on to a dealer. Kati was immediately suspected of the crime and she was well aware of it. She thought it best to make a full confession hoping all the time that the Lewis family would be forgiving. Far from that the family insisted on punishment. Accordingly Kati was sentenced to death by hanging, which was the punishment for theft in those days. She was eventually executed on Heath Common. Before the execution Kati complained about the injustice of the sentence and cursed Greenmeadow, condemning it to disappearance within a hundred years. Her curse came true; Greenmeadow is no more.

It remains to be investigated to what degree Kati's unhappy life has influenced the haunting of Greenmeadow.

Who or what lurked in the dark candle-lit cellar of Greenmeadow? It is said that an unpleasant hunchback dwelled in the cellars of the mansion. Did he sometimes leave the cellars to haunt the driveway and the garden? The unpleasant hunchback would fit the description of the ghost the Melingriffith Band encountered on the driveway: fierce, foul and awful. Was it also the fearsome hunchback that so frightened the gardener Daniel and eventually – most likely – killed him?

Tremadog
He fired his gun at the ghost
Tan-yr-Allt in Tremadog is an ancient mysterious-looking building with an illustrious history. Many tenants of rank and name used to lodge there. One of them was Percy Bysshe Shelley.

The saying is that the building has been haunted for a long time, even in Shelley's days. He once saw a ghostly face looking in through a window. Shelley made short work of it – he fired his gun at the apparition. It probably was of no use, for the ghost returned and its presence was witnessed more than a century later by Captain Livingston.

Captain Sandy Livingston and his wife lived at Tan-yr-Allt in the twentieth century. The Livingstons soon learned that the house was haunted. There was the tread of feet in the corridors upstairs where nobody should have been. Windows rattled in their frames when there was no wind and doors opened and closed moved by an invisible force.

In 1952 Mrs Livingston died and began to haunt the house. The captain saw the ghost of his deceased wife only once but he often felt her presence and heard her as did his dog.

The garden is also haunted. Captain Livingston saw the spectre of a man walking around in the garden. The phantom was clad in a long grey cloak and wore a tricorn. More than likely the man in the grey cloak is identical with the ghost that frightened Shelley by looking through the window.

Treuddyn, Flintshire
Brother Adolphus

The spook of Penyffordd Farm in Treuddyn began with the appearance of spectral graffiti on the walls of the building. One day an ancient Welsh word 'tangnefedd', which translates as religious peace, appeared on the fireplace.

From that day onwards graffiti began to appear all over the house. Many of the words had a religious connotation: *iachad* (healing), *ffydd* (faith), *gweddi* (prayer), *paderau* (rosary), *cannwyll* (candle) and *mynach* (monk). Six weeks after the death of the family's dog, *'ci'*, the Welsh for dog, appeared on a wall in the kitchen.

There may be a connection between the graffiti and a phantom monk who has shown himself to several members of the family. The monk has become so much a part of the family that he was even given a name, Brother Adophus. The monk is affectionately referred to as Brother Doli, a short form for Adolphus. Brother Doli has a good sense of humour and loves to tease visitors. When they take pictures in and around the building he often mysteriously appears on them. He also likes to influence visitors' watches by slowing them down.

A psychic who investigated the haunting believes that Brother Doli was murdered by a swordsman. According to the psychic the monk's untimely death is the cause of the spook. The year of Brother Doli's death is thought to be 1613. A date, 1610, cut into the lintel of the family's cottage proves that the building was already existent when the unfortunate monk was murdered. Brother Adolphus could have been murdered on his way to nearby Valle Crucis abbey.

Wrexham *(Wrecsam)*
Squire Yorke is about

Erddig Hall in Wrexham was built in the last quarter of the seventeenth century. The building is open to the public and is worth a visit. There is a collection of eighteenth-century furniture, porcelain, and glass on the first floor. The building also has a historic blacksmith's shop, sawmill, stable yard, carriages, laundry, bakehouse, and kitchen. Its eighteenth-century walled garden is of historic importance. And yes, it is also a gothic novel come true. If you have a love for phantom footsteps in a dark corridor and similar spectral phenomena you will be richly rewarded when you come to Erddig Hall.

It is thought that a former owner, Squire Simon Yorke, haunts Erddig Hall. The ghost was first noticed in the 1960s. A housekeeper used to spend her evenings in the kitchen of the building. She often heard phantom footsteps approaching the kitchen which she identified as Squire Yorke's footsteps.

Gwilym, a young schoolboy, drowned in the river in the late 1940s. It is thought that the wind blew his cap into the river and that he attempted to retrieve it. He fell into the river and drowned. Gwilym's ghost began to haunt the area. His presence creates an eerie atmosphere which frightens both humans and animals. The haunting seems to be centred around a bridge beside the river near Erddig. Gwilym often shows himself sitting under said bridge. He has been described as an unhappy ghost with an untidy appearance, who sobs and weeps. The boy still wears his school uniform.

5

Phantoms of the roadside

We are not alone in this world. Our ancestors thought that we were surrounded by exotic life. There were dryads, dwarves, gnomes, elves, fairies, giants, pixies and so forth. You could chance upon them on your way through a dark forest or somewhere in the mountains. Vampires and werewolves belonged to the more unsavory types of life on this planet. And, of course, there were plenty of ghosts. In bygone days a traveler would avoid certain areas because they were haunted. The general public often tends to associate ghosts uniquely and wrongly with buildings, but the ghosts of our ancestors have stubbornly refused to go away. The phantoms of the roadside are still there − and some of them are quite scary.

Abertillery, Blaenau Gwent
Who Haunts the A4046 Aber-big to Cwm Road?
It is thought that the ghost of Hosea Pope haunts the A4046 Aber-big to Cwm Road. Passers-by have frequently noticed a male ghost in old-fashioned clothes on the A4046. Many of them automatically believe to have seen the ghost of Hosea Pope who was a policeman in the early part of the twentieth century. When he died he was only thirty-four years of age and married.

Around 11pm on 14 July 1911 Pope attempted to arrest James Wise for throwing around stones on the Aber-big to Abertillery Road. Wise was a local troublemaker. A fight broke out between the two men. After a short while Pope dropped down dead. James Wise escaped but was later arrested for murder. He was cleared of the charge in a trial. Dr Kemp, who examined Pope's body at the crime scene, concluded that the policeman had died of heart failure. Nevertheless Wise was sentenced to five years' hard labour for manslaughter.

It is believed that Pope's ghost began to haunt the road on which he had died. In 1980 a local man had an encounter with the phantom. He saw the spectre standing near the Hanbury Hotel. The ghost was dressed in old-fashioned clothes and wore a top hat. The phantom stared at the man and pulled out a pocket watch. All of a sudden the screams of a woman could be heard coming from the woods near the Brondeg filling station at Cwm Big. The ghost immediately made for the woods. The man felt that he had to find out more about the mysterious man with the top hat. He decided to follow the stranger into the woods and managed to track him for a while. It came as a shock to the man when the stranger with the top hat vanished into thin air. Only then did it dawn on him that he had met the ghost of Hosea Pope.

The haunting should be seen in a critical light as there are numerous and much older supernatural legends in circulation in the area. The haunting may therefore consist of nothing more but scraps of folklore.

Even if the A4046 Aber-big to Cwm Road is truly haunted, there is circumstantial evidence to support the theory that it may not be the doing of Hosea Pope's ghost. The ghost always seems to wear a high hat or a top hat. The police did not wear that type of hat when Pope was alive. This suggests that the ghost is not Pope. On the other hand Pope may for some reason have worn his private clothes the night he died. In that case Pope could very well have worn a high hat.

Beddgelert, Gwynedd
The White Woman of the Aberglaslyn Pass
A lady in white haunts the Aberglaslyn Pass. The saying is that she is pretty and well-mannered, but one should not be blinded by her appearance and manners. An encounter with her is not desirable, for she is an harbinger of death.

It is also said that the spirit of the famous and faithful hound Gelert haunts the Aberglaslyn Pass where its tomb is thought to be. There is, however, considerable doubt whether it is an authentic tomb. This criticism is based on the observation that the tale of Gelert was unknown in the area before 1798. Some researchers argue that the tale of Gelert was introduced by David Pritchard who was the landlord of the Goat Hotel. He was also known as a good story teller. It is believed that David Pritchard placed a stone in a field and called it Gelert's Grave.

Beddgelert, Gwynedd
She climbs out of the water
About three kilometres to the north of Beddgelert is a narrow gorge, a chasm not much more than a metre wide. At the bottom of the chasm the river Colwyn snakes its way through the area. Along the edge of the steep chasm there is a place known as *Llam Trwsgl* ('clumpsy leap'). Falling into the gorge in this place meant – and still means – certain death.

Llam Trwsgl is a haunted place. It is believed that the haunting was caused by the death of a young woman. The spirit of an almost nude young beautiful lady with dripping wet hair often appears around Llam Trwsgl. Sometimes the ghost takes a different shape, and manifests itself as a young lady dressed in rustling silk.

The ghost of Llam Trwsgl goes back to an event in the nineteenth century. A young man was engaged to be married to one of the local women. Unfortunately for the young bride-to-be the man met another woman, with whom he fell in love. He kept the new relationship secret and pretended that he was still going to get married to his betrothed. Secretly he sought a way to rid himself of the now inconvenient woman without incurring the wrath of her family. As he could not come up with any practical solution he decided to murder his betrothed and to disguise the murder as an accident. Llam Trwsgl offered him the opportunity he was looking for. The young people of the area were then in the habit of jumping over the narrow chasm.

One can only guess the reason for this habit. The jump over the gap may well have the same root as the ancient custom of jumping over a fire. It was practised all over Europe. In some parts of Europe this custom is still quite alive: in Russia and Ukraine, for instance, the jump over the fire is still practised on Ivan Kupala Night. The jump is said to bring fertility to the soil, and by implication fertility to human couples. The man's bride may have had similar hopes when she jumped with her future husband over Llam Trwsgl. Different thoughts were on the mind of the man she loved so much, and he pushed her down the narrow gorge. As the banks are so steep the young woman could not pull herself out of the water and drowned. Soon after that incident her ghost began to haunt Llam Trwsgl.

Broughton, Flintshire
The phantom vicar of Broughton
The ghost of a deceased vicar troubled the vicinity of Broughton during the early 1930. The Old Warren, a deserted and tree-lined road, was then a popular walk for young courting people. Once a spooky apparition appeared to a couple of lovers, a tall man dressed in the black garb of a clergyman. With a disdainful look on his face he slipped past the frightened lovers.

The ghostly clergyman also appeared to another couple. As the lovers were about to depart the ghost of the clergyman manifested itself and floated past the couple's motorbike, causing the light of the bike to go on and off.

According to more recent sources the phantom vicar is still around. He still patrols Old Warren, although he seems to have slightly altered his modus operandi. The saying is that the vicar now peers into parked cars.

Bwlchgwyn, Wrexham
The ghostly army of the valley of Nant y Ffrith

It is thought that a phantom army haunts the Valley of Nant y Ffrith near Bwlchgwyn. The haunting of Bwlchgwyn was first recorded in autumn of the year 1602. A large medieval army with banners and horses appeared in the valley of Nant y Ffrith in front of several witnesses. It is believed that the spectral army consists of between 2000 and 3000 soldiers.

Connah's Quay, Flintshire
Nora visits Wepre Park

For generations the dead pets of Wepre Hall in Connah's Quay were buried in a plot of land in Wepre Park. This part of Wepre Park became known as 'The Dogs' Graves'. It is believed that the ghosts of the dead dogs sometimes leave their graves to haunt the area.

A man from Shotton had an encounter with the phantom dogs one night. He was walking his dog when all of a sudden a pack of dogs rushed towards them. The dogs ranged from small to big but uncannily they were uniform in colour. When the light of the moon shone on the dogs the man realised that all of them were grey. Quite untypical of dogs, the pack moved about in silence, completely ignoring the walker and his dog, and made straight for a path which leads to the pet cemetery of Wepre Park. When they had reached the entrance they vanished. Of a sudden the pet cemetery reverberated with eerie howling.

The haunting of the spectral dogs is not the only supernatural occurrence in the area. A phantasmal nun sometimes shows herself to passers-by in Wepre Park.

On a fine summer night while on his way home an angler saw a young boy fleeing from Wepre Pool. The youngster appeared to be extremely scared so the angler stopped and questioned him. The boy explained that he had run away from a hideous old nun that lurked in a hedge. The boy was so terrified that he had left his fishing gear behind. The kindly angler offered to help him retrieve the equipment and to investigate the hedge. Just as they reached the spot where the boy had dropped his fishing gear the angler became aware of a dark, receding shadow in the hedge.

Another angler came face to face with the phantom nun. He described the ghost as a nun dressed in white. The man would probably have thought nothing of the encounter had the nun not been hovering in the air behind him.

The nun also appeared to a couple of lovers. One evening they went for a walk in Wepre Park when they heard a humming sound. They followed the sound and soon a waterfall came into sight. A female ghost was walking on top of the waterfall. The sight of the phantom frightened the couple so much that they turned around and fled. The woman's boyfriend claims to have felt cold hands on his shoulder. Had the ghost caught up with the lovers and touched the boyfriend's shoulder?

The presence of the phantom nun can be easily explained. It is known that there was once a convent at Wepre. The fate and name of the spectral nun are also known. Her name is Nora. Local legend has it that she found a baby that was left on the doorsteps of the convent. She took in the baby and cared for it. One day she took the baby to Wepre Brook to wash it. The baby slipped out of her hands and the current swept it away. The infant surely drowned. The incident so upset the nun that she drowned herself in the Wepre Brook some time later. Her spirit began to haunt the area.

According to another legend Nora had an affair with a monk. She became pregnant and gave birth to a child. In order to cover up her illicit affair she murdered the child. Her end was tragic. One account, as seen, states that she drowned. However, there is an alternative version in which she was decapitated. The truth is most likely that Nora really had an affair with a monk and that she murdered her baby. There is circumstantial evidence to support this theory. It seems unreal that the nun should have taken a new-born baby to Wepre Brook to wash it in the brook's cold waters. Nora would have known that babies do not bear cold well. The assumption that Nora flung the infant in the brook to rid herself of the evidence of her illicit affair does not seem too far-fetched. Another bit of circumstantial evidence is the presence of a headless phantom monk in Wepre Park. The suggestion that the ghostly monk was Nora's lover seems realistic. For violating his vows he was decapitated.

It appears that the death of the monk and Nora's end became confused. As already seen, there are conflicting accounts of Nora's death in circulation. However, the existence of the headless monk-ghost would suggest that it was the monk who was decapitated and not the nun. Nora always appears with her head on her shoulders. She therefore really seems to have drowned. Her death was most likely suicide.

Crickhowell (Crughywel), Powys
Tally-ho
One night in June when the Rev Thomas travelled from Crickhowell to Llangynidr he was attacked by a particularly

violent ghost in filthy clothes. The clothes looked rather like the wrappings around a mummy. The phantom had a haggard appearance and glowing eyes. When the spirit became aware of Mr Thomas it began to chase him. The clergyman was exceedingly frightened. He managed to escape to Llangynidr. When Mr Thomas mentioned his encounter with the spectre the villagers told him that a man who fitted the description of the ghost once lived in the neighbourhood. He had long since died. Alive, as in death, the ghost had an unpleasant character.

Denbighshire
The centurion of Denbigh Moors

Legend has it that a Roman centurion haunts Denbigh Moors. It is thought that he died in battle. The violent death of the centurion is believed to be the cause of the haunting.

The centurion leaves his grave on moonlit nights. His bright armour gleams in the moonshine. The appearance of the ancient Roman is truly majestic and impressive. The centurion is history come to life again. It is therefore tempting to investigate this particular haunting. Studying it may come at a cost. It could lead to the loss of one's life. According to local tradition the ghost of the ancient Roman is a harbinger of death. When the centurion arises from his tomb and crosses the path of an unsuspecting passer-by the seed of death is sown.

Ewenni, Vale of Glamorgan
A Sinister Secret

It is thought that the ghost of a lady in white haunts White Lady's Meadow and White Lady's Lane between Ewenni and Bridgend. A sinister secret condemns her to a spectral existence in the area.

Long ago a house stood somewhere between White Lady's Meadow and White Lady's Lane. The building has not survived the passage of time. The house harboured a terrible secret. A crime was committed in the building. The details of the incident were lost over the decades. It is still known that a woman was involved in the crime. Driven by guilt she returned from the world beyond to haunt the site of the crime. She often shows herself on the meadow where her house once stood and also in a nearby lane. Lane and meadow were named after the spook, White Lady's Meadow and White Lady's Lane. Quite frequently she just stands on the meadow and points towards Ewenny or wrings her hands in despair.

Once a man made an attempt to help the lady in white. He approached her and was told that it was in his power to redeem her. All he had to do was to hold the woman's hands firmly for a while and release them on her command. The man took her by the hands but he became distracted when a dog barked and released her accidentally. She wailed in pain and explained to the man that she was bound for another seven years because of his failure. After that she disappeared.

The White Lady's comment is ambiguous. She told the man that she was bound for another seven years. The meaning of this could be that the haunting was coming to its natural end with the passage of the seventh year. Her comment can also be interpreted differently. It may well mean that she had to wait for another seven years before she could approach another person with the request to have her hands held tightly.

Flint
She lost her love in Cornist Park
In the legend of Cornist Park in Flint a young woman fell in love with a man and became engaged to him. As a pledge of love they exchanged engagement rings. The woman's father did not care much for the young man. It is said that the lady's enraged father threw the engagement ring in the brushwood

203

of the park. The young woman died before the ring was found. Her ghost has returned from the realm of the dead to search for her ring.

Gower, Swansea
The phantom four-in-hand on Rhosili Beach

Squire Mansell belonged to an ancient family of the area around Rhosili. Local legends describe him as a rather tyrannical and greedy man.

One night, when a shipwreck with a cargo of gold was found on Rhosili beach he drove his black four-in-hand down to the site of the wreckage at breakneck speed. He chased away the villagers who were helping themselves to some of the gold and loaded the treasure on his coach. After that the squire searched the houses of the villagers and confiscated the little bit of gold they had taken. He was then in possession of the whole treasure.

Mansell went abroad and squandered the gold. He returned empty-handed to Rhosili and began to search the beach in the hope of finding more treasure, a hope that never came true. Mansell continued his treasure hunt even after his death. On stormy nights his ghostly four-in-hand can sometimes be seen chasing up Rhosili beach.

Llangennith, Swansea
From the grave to the Main Road

The ghost manifests itself above a grave. The scene is set for a terrifying haunting. Dressed in a long gauzy white funerary shirt she wandered around in the graveyard.

A group of surfers had a brush with a lady in white in the village of Llangennith. They were surprised to see a lady in gauzy white clothes walking around in the cemetery of Llangennith Church.

The White Lady was seen again somewhat later. She was

then travelling along the main road between Rhosili and Llangennith.

It is believed that the haunting is caused by the presence of an ancient well. In many ancient cultures wells used to be sacred and were protected by spirit guardians. Be it as it may, the case is open to speculation.

It is known that the ghost of a clergyman, Rev. John Ponsonby Lucas, haunts Llangennith. His spectre has been sighted in a number of places in the village, especially around Llangennith Church. Mr Lucas was not popular with his congregation because of his high-handed attitude towards his flock. Eventually many parishioners stayed away from his services.

Is the phantom lady in white one of Mr Lucas's victims? Did she need spiritual guidance and consolation but could not find it in Mr Lucas's church? Did she therefore come back from the world beyond to haunt the area where she was left without help and comfort?

Llangrannog, Ceredigion
The return of a sailor
The ghost of a deceased sailor, Huw Pugh, often shows himself on the beach of Llangrannog. One evening Huw appeared to Jennifer when she was walking on the beach. He stood by the sea staring at the waves. At first Jennifer was not even aware that she had an encounter with a ghost. When she came closer to Huw she realised that he was dressed in an old-fashioned sailor suit which struck her as strange. Jennifer was even more amazed when the sailor vanished before her eyes. She decided to make enquiries in the village and was told that she had seen the ghost of Huw Pugh, a seaman that died in the area in the eighteenth century.

Llanrhidian, Swansea
The warrior of Arthur's Stone
It is believed that a stately figure in shinning armour haunts the area around Cefyn Bryn. The haunting only occurs on a night when the moon is full. Then the ancient warrior leaves his tomb, which is supposed to be under Arthur's Stone. The figure can then be seen making his way towards Llandrhidian.

Marford, Wrexham
The corpse left the coffin
The ghost of Margaret Blackbourne has returned to the village of Marford. Her true name is seldom used in Marford. She is commonly referred to as 'Lady Blackbird'.

Ancient lore teaches that a supernatural creature should not be called by its true name for this will inevitably conjure it up. Accordingly, demons like the devil have various nicknames like, for instance, Old Nick. The same concept appears to be behind the re-naming of Margaret Blackbourne.

Margaret was married to George Blackbourne, who was a violent man and drank excessively. He was also a notorious womaniser. It is believed that he murdered Margaret in 1713 at Rofft Hall, which was the home of the family. The saying is that he pushed her down the stairs in a drunken rage when she mentioned his womanising.

There is also an alternative version in which George murdered his wife in nearby Pant Wood. Be it as it may, George got away unpunished because the coroner who held the inquest was closely related to him. The coroner's verdict was death by accident.

Six month after the murder George married again and went to live with his new wife at Rofft Hall. It was an ill-fated marriage. Husband and wife never had a minute of peace because Margaret returned from the grave to haunt their house. Local legend has it that her corpse clawed its way through coffin and soil and made for Rofft Hall. On the way to her former home she would knock on each window in the village. The sight of her pale face with its dead eyes would terrify the inhabitants of Marford.

Back home in Rofft Hall Margaret would roam around in the building's long corridors moaning all the time. She would also appear in the wedding chamber and stay there until dawn. The haunting drove the couple out of their home. They moved to Trevalyn Hall in Rossett, but to their great dismay the corpse followed them.

It is said that a priest managed to bind the corpse. Unfortunately, he failed to exorcise Margaret's ghost. Her ghost is still at large in Marford. The fear of the phantom woman caused the villagers to fix crosses to the walls of their cottages. A number of windows were even given the shape of crosses as a safeguard against the haunting.

Merthyr Mawr, Bridgend
Do not cross the Ogmore River

In bygone days waggoners and horsemen used to ford the river Ogmore near Merthyr Mawr during the summer when the water level was low. After heavy rainfall the river was avoided because the increase in water made it wild and dangerous.

On a fine summer evening a teamster attempted to cross the Ogmore, not heeding the warning he had been given by a man earlier in the day. He was told that there had been heavy rainfall in the hilly regions around Bridgend. As a result of the downpour the river carried more water than usual and it had gathered great speed on its way down the hills. Nonetheless the waggoner drove his team of horses into the Ogmore. Soon the current tossed about the heavy waggon. Teamster and horses fought in vain against the forces of the river. They were carried away into the sea, never to be seen again.

Local legend has it that the ghost of the waggoner appears as a warning when there is an imminent danger in the area. He can then be seen with his waggon and team of horses.

Mold, Flintshire
The phantom warrior of Goblin Hill
The Golden Spectre of Goblin Hill (*'Bryn yr Ellyllon'* in Welsh) is one of the best-known ghost stories in Wales.

Goblin Hill is located in Pentre, which is the eastern part of Mold. In that location there once existed a prehistoric dolmen tomb which was levelled in the nineteenth century. The tomb contained the most substantial prehistoric gold artefact ever discovered in Europe, an elaborately ornamented sheet of gold which the owner would have worn in the fashion of a cape. The tomb was the final resting place of an ancient warrior whose ghost haunted the area. The ghost is referred to as Brenin yr Allt ('king of the hill'). This king from the ghost realm is a tall and stately warrior clad in golden armour.

Some years before the destruction of the tomb a woman saw the ghost on her way home. Although night had fallen she could see the warrior clearly for his golden armour gleamed in a ghostly light. He stepped forth from a cluster of trees and disappeared in the tomb. The woman's encounter with the ghost is of vital importance as it took place a long time before the golden cape was discovered. At that time nobody knew of the golden cape.

A good number of critics argue that the destruction of the tomb put an end to the spook. There is evidence to the contrary.

The student John Smith had an encounter with the phantom on his way home one night in December 1988. When he came near the site of the tomb John noticed footsteps behind him. He halted and peered in the darkness in an attempt to make out who was coming after him but there did not seem to be anybody around. To John's great dismay the footsteps of the pursuer had also fallen silent, which meant that he could not even locate the uncanny stalker acoustically. As soon as he resumed walking the phantom footsteps reappeared. John turned around several times trying to catch out the pursuer but there was no one in sight. In the end he became so scared that he ran away at full speed.

Mold, Flintshire
The ghost of Goblin Well

On the road to Gwernaffield about a kilometre and a half outside Mold there used to be an old well called *Ffynnon Ellyllon* ('goblin well'). The area around the well is thought to be haunted. A headless lady in white sometimes appears to passers-by.

One night she showed herself to a somewhat inebriated young man who was on his way home. Her face was shadowed by a hood. She asked the man to accompany her for a while because she feared the dangers of the night. He could not refuse such a request. The hooded lady walked quietly beside him. Purely by chance he caught a glimpse of what was hidden under the hood. The man nearly fainted when he discovered that the hood was completely empty; the lady in the white dress was headless. When she realised that her secret was uncovered she pulled her severed head forth from her cloak where it had been hidden all the time. The young man tried to run away but found that he was unable to do so. The phantom had some supernatural power over him. She explained to her captive that she had died long ago and that she could only be redeemed if a certain necklace were put around her headless neck. If this happened head and body would be united again. The necklace was part of a treasure hidden in the area which the young man was to dig up. She only claimed the necklace for herself. At some stage during the conversation with the ghost the man sneezed whereupon he is said to have uttered 'Heaven keep me'. The mention of the sacred phrase broke the enchantment of the spirit and the lady in white disappeared.

It is believed that the lady ghost is still around and that she is unlikely ever to feel lonely because the region appears to be haunted by hundreds of phantom warriors.

In 1997 a huntsman was hunting in the woods near Gwernaffield Road when he heard the rumbling of horse-drawn wagons and the clanking of clashing swords coming from a nearby field. The noise of the swords was followed by the death screams of fighting men. The hunter decided to explore the area. Although it was late at night he could see everything around him clearly in the light of the full moon. Nonetheless he was unable to locate the source of the noise. Of a sudden it dawned on the huntsman that he was in a haunted place. The thought of being surrounded by invisible phantoms scared him profoundly. His normally brave dog was also exceedingly frightened and remained at his master's side all the time.

Huntsman and dog made good their escape as quickly as possible and have not been back ever since.

Mold, Flintshire
The happy ghost of Moel Famau
It is believed that the ghost of a young lady in a blue dress haunts the hill of Moel Famau near Mold.

Contrary to what is commonly believed not all ghosts lead a sad and miserable existence. Some ghosts come across as merry and happy. The lady in blue of Moel Famau belongs to this class of happy ghosts. Whenever she materialises on the hill she appears to be dancing merrily to some inaudible tune. Her cheerfulness even has a soothing effect on bystanders. The phantom lady looks so real that she is never taken for a ghost at first glance. Her true identity is revealed when she disappears from one second to another.

The roots of the spook of Moel Famau could possibly be found in the ancient fairy hauntings of Celtic folklore. The behaviour of the dancing lady is somewhat atypical of a ghosts. It fits in better with the character of the Tylwyth Teg, the fairies. They are known for their love for dancing and singing. The lady of Moel Famau may therefore not really be a true ghost.

Nannerch, Flintshire
The hooded lady of Nannerch
It is thought that the ghost of a woman in a long black hooded gown haunts the road leading up to the Royal Oak Pub in Nannerch. The phantom woman always wears a hood that completely conceals her face. She also appears to be looking down as if she were studying the ground in front of her. The hooded lady has shown herself to a considerable number of passers-by over the last century.

In the latter part of the twentieth century Luke Thomas and a friend had an encounter with the ghostly woman. They were on their way to the Royal Oak when she suddenly stepped out of a hedge by the wayside. As the woman appeared to be real enough they only realised that they had met a ghost when the lady in black vanished before their eyes.

In the 1950s the lady in black showed herself to a police constable. He was on night duty walking towards Wheeler Hill when he saw a woman coming towards him. The constable was surprised to see her disappearing behind a hedge. Out of curiosity he flashed the light of his strong torch at the hedge and searched it but he found no trace of the woman.

Around 1945 a man was cycling home from work one night when the hooded woman appeared out of nowhere directly in front of him which forced him to brake so hard that he fell from his bike. The phantom woman then made for the hedge where she disappeared.

There are even surviving witness statements from the nineteenth century. A man was on his way home from a party when his horse suddenly became very nervous. There was a drop of temperature and a white mist appeared on the road through which he was forced to ride as there was no way around it. When he looked over his shoulder he saw the lady in black disappearing into a hedge.

While the hedge features strongly in the haunting it did not exist during the lifetime of the lady in black. It is of a more recent date. The site of the hedge was once occupied by a gate that led to the lady's cottage. The remains of this cottage could still be seen in the 1930s. Thus when the woman in black steps through the hedge she is treading the ground where her garden gate used to be. The haunting then takes place on and around the site where she once lived. It is not known for sure why she haunts her former home. Some of the witnesses have tried to reason out the cause of the haunting. They concluded that the woman probably stepped out of the gate and onto the road where she was knocked down by a cart or horse. The accident would then have caused her death and the subsequent haunting. The observation that she appears with her head bent to the ground lends some support to this theory. Looking to the ground or even reading something, she would not have seen an approaching vehicle.

Neath
Needles, pins and cockles
In 1986 the spectre of a stout woman was seen near the bandstand in Victoria Gardens in Neath. The woman's clothes are covered with lace decorations and are in the style of the gypsies of the nineteenth century. It is therefore believed that she belonged to the 'Merched Y Mera'. The 'Merched Y Mera'

were Romani women whose children always took the maternal surname. In the nineteenth century they used to travel through south Wales where they sold their goods from wicker-baskets. The ghost also carries such a basket.

Since her first appearance in 1986 the woman has been seen a few times trying to sell needles, pins and cockles from her basket. There is a certain pattern to the haunting. The woman would hold out her basket to passers-by attempting to sell her wares. Unfortunately her prospective clients never seem to be aware of her and therefore always ignore her. After several fruitless attempts the ghost disappears.

Newport
Squire Thomas of Redwick
The thirsty ghost of Squire Thomas troubles the village of Redwick. The squire had quite a taste for cider which he retained even after his death.

One night he was on his way home inebriated with cider. He fell into a ditch full of water but was too drunk to save himself. His ghost began to trouble a local cider brewer. Squire Thomas used to visit the brewer to drink his cider. The brewer may well have put up with the loss of a few jars of cider, but what annoyed him was that the ghost regularly opened the taps of the barrels to let the cider drip out. As time went on the spirit became bolder. Thomas began to appear in the village. His preferred haunt was a spot opposite Rose Cottage. At last the village decided to get rid of the troublesome ghost. A minister read the exorcism. The squire simply ignored the minister's efforts. In another version the ghost was exorcised by a group of clergymen.

The saying is that the thirsty squire is still around and that he has been seen recently

Pontypool, Torfaen
A day with dear Juan White

Juan White was a local woman with a rather malevolent personality. When she was dead her ghost returned to haunt a geographically wide area. She was seen in the mountains around Brynithel between Abertillery and Pontypool.

Some details of her life have survived. It is known that she lived in a cottage on Lasgarn Hill which is near Pontypool. Her humble appearance did not reveal her true nature. She looked very much like any other old woman of her time and age. According to a surviving description she was a poor old crone whose clothes were the colour of ash. She wore a four-cornered hat and almost always carried a milk vessel in her hands. Juan's ghost took some pleasure in leading travellers astray. She would appear to travellers that were disorientated and in distress. She always looked like a being of flesh and blood and not at all like a ghost. They would see her walking along purposefully and thus automatically assume that she was a local and that it was therefore safe to follow her. It was a fatal mistake to hope that Juan would lead them out of the wilderness. The ghost used to lead the travellers into boggy areas where quite a few of them must have undoubtedly perished. Sometimes Juan did not even deem it necessary to appear in person. She found that shouting and hollering was enough to mislead wayfarers that were not familiar with the geography of the area.

At other times she would mysteriously travel in a coach. The rumbling of the coach and the horses could then clearly be heard.

John ap John had an encounter with Juan on Milfraen Mountain. Juan's voice seemed to come from all sides. At last a coach approached from behind. John knew that this was quite impossible for no earthly coach could access the wilderness of Milfraen Mountain. Probably half expecting to see a horse-drawn hearse John decided that he did not want to have a look at the coach. He flung himself in a ditch where he hid himself face down in the mud.

The ghost also struck around Llangattock near Crickhowell. One night Robert Williams was on his way home to Llangattock when he lost his way coming across the mountains. In the darkness he made out the shape of an elderly woman some paces ahead of him. He addressed the woman hoping to receive help from her but he was given no answer. He assumed that the woman was deaf and had not heard him so he began to walk faster to catch up with her. However fast he walked the woman always remained ahead of him. Finally he run. As a result of this he stumbled and fell. This seemed to amuse the woman in front of him. Juan turned around and laugh maliciously.

At this point Robert Williams remembered the stories he had heard about Juan White. He then realised that he had met her ghost. He got up on his feet, drew his knife, and brandished it at Juan upon which she disappeared instantly. When the spectre was gone Robert became aware that he had been led into a bog. Fortunately he was able to work his way out.

Some argue that it was the presence of iron that drove away the spirit. They are guided in their belief by the old legend that fairies fear iron. Juan is a ghost and not a fairy. She therefore has nothing to fear from iron. It was probably Robert's fearlessness that scared away the phantom.

Juan seems to have been rather quiet for a few decades, but in 1986 Juan came back again. On 25 March 1986 the *South Wales Argus* published an article on Juan White. A young couple from Pontygaseg had an encounter with Juan's ghost. Juan appeared in front of their car and began to walk at a slow pace thus blocking the road. Eventually the couple got past Juan and made an attempt to speak with her. How surprised they were when she vanished before their eyes!

Juan was seen even more recently, on 18 July 2004. On that date she appeared to a couple who also heard the sound of her horses shortly before she manifested herself. Juan was clearly visible but they never saw the horses.

In view of such news it can hardly be argued that the good old days are gone for ever! The old girl is back in town again!

Port Talbot, Neath
The White Lady of St Mary's Churchyard

Towards the end of the nineteenth century Afan Castle was demolished and houses were built on the former castle ground. The memory of the old castle lives on in the name of the road where the houses stand, Castle Street in Port Talbot.

It is thought that the demolished castle was haunted and that the ghost has survived the destruction of the building. A lady in white sometimes shows herself in the area where the castle once stood.

It is believed that the woman in white is Lady Margaret who was the mother of Sir John of Afan. But a number of researchers have questioned the identify of the ghost and offered a different solution. They believe that the lady in the white dress is the ghost of Jane de Afan who was the last occupant of Afan Castle. Lady Jane would have had a good reason to haunt her former residence. It is thought that one of the reasons that causes a haunting is great discontent. This aspect applies to Lady Jane. When she married an English knight she automatically lost her heritage. Strictly speaking, she betrayed her bloodline which would be a strong enough reason to cause a haunting. Be it as it may, a silent lady in an immaculately white dress has frequently been seen near St Mary's churchyard which is the site where the castle once stood.

Prestatyn, Denbighshire
The phantom lady of Old Rhyl Road

The spectre of an old woman haunts the winding back road to Rhyl from Prestatyn and Dyserth, a road known in the area as the Old Rhyl Road. She was sighted for the first time in the 1960s.

On a stormy and rainy night Anne Williams and a friend were driving along the Old Rhyl Road when she noticed a woman walking along the road in the downpour. They decided to offer the old lady a lift and reversed the car. Soon they reached the stretch of the road where the old lady should have been but there was no one at all. This was somewhat of a mystery. The road was flanked by high hedges and it appeared to be improbable that the elderly lady had climbed over them. Anne soon forgot the incident.

Some time after the strange occurrence on the Old Rhyl Road, Anne got married. One evening she mentioned her encounter with the elderly lady to her husband and was surprised to learn that he had met her too. Her husband knew for sure that the Old Rhyl Road was haunted. He had seen the old lady a few times when she was still alive and also after her death. The phantom woman appeared to Anne's husband when he was travelling to Rhyl on the Old Rhyl Road on a rainy night. He stopped to give the old woman a lift. How amazed he was when he realised that she had vanished. He still remembers that the old woman wore a white raincoat.

The ghost of the old lady in white seems to be quite active. Four shift workers were driving home one night on the Old Rhyl Road when they sighted the spectre. The White Lady stepped on the road right in front of their car. They clearly felt the impact of the collision and stopped all at once to help the accident victim. When they got out of the car they discovered to their great surprise that the woman had disappeared.

The White Lady was witnessed as recently as in 2005.

Witnesses saw her partially covered by a wall on 1 January 2005. She was seen leaning over the wall and vanished all of a sudden.

Tenby, Pembrokeshire
Don't lose your head!

When faced with the haunting between Tenby and Sampson Cross one should keep one's cool or, at least, not lose one's head ...

This part of Tenby is haunted by a phantom coach pulled by headless horses. The coachman follows the fashion; he is also headless. The coach carries a lady who does her best to keep up the tradition: she, too, has no head.

The coach appears only during the night and literally disappears with a big bang; it explodes and vanishes from sight. The haunting has been described as very frightening.

Trelawnyd, Flintshire
The lady and the general

Local legend has it that Boudicca, queen of the Iceni, who so bravely fought the Roman oppressors in AD 60 was buried on Gop Carn in the vicinity of Trelawnyd. It is thought that the bellicose queen sometimes leaves her tomb for the occasional foray into the surrounding area. Well, that's all right, resting in a tomb appears to be a rather dull affair. Why should she not have some fun?

There is also a Roman general and many Roman legionaries in the area. These Roman foot-soldiers were first seen in 1938. Since then they have shown themselves to the odd passer-by. As for the Roman general, a witness returning from Dyserth had an encounter with him. The spectral general proudly sat on a white horse and held a drawn sword in his hand. When the moon disappeared behind a cloud the general vanished. Maybe he was on a date to see Boudicca? Let us hope for the best.

Wrexham
The ghost of Brymbo Hall continues

The tragic events at Brymbo Hall began with an arranged marriage. The owner of Brymbo Hall forced his daughter to marry a man who she did not love. Though the actual wedding day was still many months in the future the arranged marriage changed the young woman's nature completely. She became sulky and sad. She took to retiring to a small room near the roof where she bemoaned her fate. The young lady shed many a secret tear in those lonely hours in the small room.

When she completed the twenty-first year of her life a ball was held to celebrate the event. Maybe the ball was also meant to uplift her spirit. Quite to the contrary, the young woman burst into tears during the ball and rushed out of the room. She hurried to her refuge near the roof of Brymbo Hall where she had spent so many unhappy hours. Gripped by utter desperation the young woman decided to end her life. She fashioned a noose and hung herself. Meanwhile, the rest of the family and their guests believed that there was nothing seriously wrong with the young lady because she had behaved in that manner many times before. The general feeling was that she was going to re-emerge from her secret hiding place in a short while. When this did not happen a maidservant was sent to fetch her. The unfortunate maidservant found the dead body of her young mistress.

The violent death of the young woman caused her spirit to be restless. Brymbo Hall began to experience a vicious haunting. Ghostly forces threw open doors and windows, and sudden drops in temperature plagued the residents of the building. The ghost of the young lady began to appear in Brymbo Hall.

The room where she took her life was so haunted that it came to be known as the 'Ghost Room'. It is said that the haunting was so powerful that all pets would shun the Ghost

Room. The windows in the room would never stay closed even when secured with string.

The young lady's ghost was so powerful that it could even leave the building to haunt the road leading up to Brymbo Hall. The road was consequently referred to as the 'Ghost Road'

In the 1950s the building was demolished but the haunting of Brymbo Hall continued. The ghost still haunts the area where Brymbo Hall once stood, in particular the road. Numerous witnesses have seen the phantom on the road. The ghost seems to be subject to the passage of time. The appearance of the ghost has changed, and now looks like an old woman.